FROM IDEA TO BUILDING

Issues in Architecture

FROM IDEA TO BUILDING
Issues in Architecture

Michael Brawne

Butterworth Architecture
An imprint of Butterworth-Heinemann Ltd
Linacre House, Jordan Hill, Oxford OX2 8DP

 PART OF REED INTERNATIONAL BOOKS

OXFORD   LONDON   BOSTON
MUNICH   NEW DELHI   SINGAPORE   SYDNEY
TOKYO   TORONTO   WELLINGTON

First published 1992

© Butterworth-Heinemann Ltd 1992

British Library Cataloguing in Publication Data
Brawne, Michael
    From idea to building: issues in architecture.
    I. Title
    729

ISBN 0 7506 1271 1

Library of Congress Cataloguing in Publication Data
Brawne, Michael.
    From idea to building: issues in architecture/Michael Brawne.
        p.   cm.
    Includes bibliographical references and index.
    ISBN 0 7506 1271 1
    1. Architectural design.   I. Title.
    NA2750.B66   1991
    720—dc20   91–26041
                                                    CIP

Composition by Genesis Typesetting, Laser Quay, Rochester, Kent
Printed and bound in Great Britain

a critical view of the assumptions
which influence initial design decisions
and
of the processes of development from
inception to inhabited building
together with
an analysis of the general
implications of the design process

Contents

Introduction

The word 'issues' in the title of this essay is used in the sense in which it suggests subjects of general concern. The term is taken to have the meaning which C. Wright Mills gives it in *The Sociological Imagination*, where he draws an important distinction between 'troubles', which are a private matter, and 'issues', which 'transcend the local environment' and are 'a public matter'. Architectural issues are therefore discussed in the way in which they affect both architects and those who live with the work of architects – namely most of us. Architecture is assumed to be a matter of public interest and a matter of general relevance; a significant element of the world in which we live and an important clue by which we are remembered.

Architecture can indeed never be a hermetic subject. It relates to the general world of ideas and actions and is continually influenced by these. I believe it also to be a discipline which is itself sufficiently crucial – and interesting – for it to exert a reciprocal influence on the world at large. Much of this essay can perhaps be read not only as a discussion of architecture, but I hope equally as an investigation of some quite general problems which are illustrated by a case study of architectural issues. Important amongst these would be the question of how we operate in a domain in which we are continually surrounded by the effects of the past and in which these must play an important role while the main concerns of that domain are, however, not with how things are or were but, as in the case of all design, with how they ought to be.

As a result parts of the essay deal with ideas outside the realm of architecture. These are discussed because they are thought to be important in their own right and are, at the same time, believed to have relevance to the way in which we think about architectural problems. Principal among these are the writings of Sir Karl Popper. My primary debt is therefore to the published work of Karl Popper and I can only hope that he will not think that my compression of many of his expositions does grave injustice to his meanings or that my extension of his viewpoint into architecture is unwarranted.

Crucial to Sir Karl's work is the notion of conjecture and refutation; it is in fact embodied in the title of one of his books. I am therefore extremely grateful to Professor Sir Leslie Martin who in 1964 invited me to come and teach at the Department of Architecture of the University of Cambridge and thus made it possible for me to combine architectural practice with the need to face the challenge of students and of members of staff to the views I may have been putting forward. I owe a considerable debt to the many students with whom I have worked in the intervening years and to my colleagues on the staff with whom I have taught and with whom I have both agreed and disagreed. This process of critical discussion was in no way interrupted when I accepted the chair of architecture at the University of Bath in 1978 and has been particularly extended with my colleagues Edmund Happold, Professor of Building Engineering, and Peter Smithson, visiting Professor in Architecture.

Although I may have at the time shown some reluctance to be persuaded, I am now delighted that in February 1964 Royston Landau succeeded in convincing me to present a paper on Popper at a seminar at the Architectural Association and thus made it essential for me to read Popper's writings more carefully and to consider their relevance to architecture. My initial interest had been stimulated by some talks given by William W. Bartley III a year earlier. In a very similar way I am glad that Professor A. M. Vogt asked me to take part in a symposium at the ETH in Zurich in December 1974 and as a result made it necessary for me to look at the work of Gottfried Semper much more closely. Semper had until then been for me, as I think for many others brought up on architectural history books written in English, a very shadowy figure.

Architectural ideas, however, eventually need more than discussion in a seminar or over the drawing board in the studio; they require the stimulus and essential discipline of being translated into buildings. I owe a debt therefore to all those with whom I have been involved in the design and execution of building projects and who have thus also influenced my architectural ideas: to the late Leo de Syllas of Architects' Co-Partnership in whose office I first worked; to Sir Denys Lasdun who always generously insisted on analysing and discussing the general aspects of particular problems and in whose office I worked at the time of the design of the new University of East Anglia; to Colin St John Wilson, until recently Professor of Architecture at the University of Cambridge, with whom I have collaborated on a number of projects; to my wife, Charlotte Baden-Powell, with whom I have worked for many years on a number of designs; and to those in my office who have been my colleagues and with whom I have engaged in day-to-day discussion of problems: Bob Allies, Selçuk Avci, Jane Bruce Brooker, Michael Gold, Adam Hardy, Michael Heber-Percy, Richard Lavington, Bernard Parker, Anthony Perry, Martin Raper, Paul Simpson, Rick Swann, Phil Tabor, Garry Taylor, David Turnbull, Peter Wilkins, Godela von Xylander.

I also owe an indirect but very real debt to Unesco, which sent me on a number of month-long missions that provided extended and uninterrupted evenings in which to write. The first notes were thus made in Colombo while designing the National Library of Sri Lanka, sections were written in San'a in the North Yemen and Islamabad in Pakistan and some of the later portions in Maputo in Mozambique. This distance from the daily preoccupations of practice and teaching may also perhaps be reflected in a discussion of architecture in relation to much more general questions about the nature of design and its importance.

Background

1

The name of Bernard Maybeck does not appear
prominently in most books of architectural history.
Yet he was undoubtedly one of the great architects of
the San Francisco Bay Region and as such influential
over a much wider area. The omission may have
something to do with geography and the notoriously
parochial outlook of historians, or it may be due to
the equally narrow stylistic outlook which has
defined the so-called important in modern architecture. Yet what is fascinating about Maybeck is that he
too emerged from the mainstream of European
architecture and went ahead with his Californian
contemporaries to develop a style for his time: the
avowed aim of the entire modern movement.

Maybeck, together with a handful of other
architects who were working on the West Coast in
the early years of the century, elaborated a way of
building in the benign climate of California which
was both innovatory and traditional. Their starting
point was the free-standing house, a form already
well established in the American tradition, which had
recently received stimulating modifications in the
new Chicago suburbs. In the immediately preceding
decades Frank Lloyd Wright, Walter Burley Griffin
and others had restructured the villa into what was to
be at the same time a middle-class home and an
eminently usable work of art. It was part of the great
resurgence of architectural ideas which took place in
Chicago in the last years of the nineteenth and the
beginning of the twentieth century and which sprang
from a combination of great talent and equally great
opportunity. Chicago was the boom city – rail
interchange, cattle market, growing commercial
centre, expanding centre of higher education – which
had also lost large sections of its central area in the
fire of 1871. New building was not a luxury but part
of its clearly inevitable growth.

A few years later the conditions were very similar
on the West Coast. The frontier had reached the
Pacific and a land with a Mediterranean climate. This
and the earlier discovery of gold in 1848 brought a
new population. And then in 1906 earthquake and
fire virtually devastated all that existed of San
Francisco. New construction was here, as in the

1 *Bernard Maybeck*
First Church of Christ Scientist,
Berkeley, California, 1910–12

2 Greene and Greene (Charles
Sumner Greene and Henry Mather
Greene)
David B Gamble House, Pasadena,
Cal. 1908

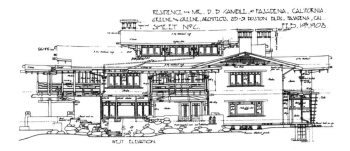

Middle West, again a necessity. Maybeck and his contemporaries – Greene and Greene working in Southern California, Irving Gill and others – took that other long-rooted American tradition of timber construction (well suited, as in Japan, to an earthquake zone) and modified it from one of studs and boarded planes to an often more open construction in which the individual pieces of wood became more defined and thus more obvious: an architecture of assembled sticks. They began to create a new style. At the same time they experimented with reinforced concrete and both Maybeck and Gill made important innovations.

But behind these changes lay not only the years of building which had taken place in America during the previous three centuries – the colonial tradition of the East Coast stemming from the European Renaissance, the work of the Chicago School itself, influenced by the innovations introduced by Richardson

3 Irving Gill
Women's Club, La Jolla, Cal. 1913
concrete tilt slab system

9

4 *Bernard Maybeck*
First Church of Christ Scientist,
Berkeley, Cal. 1910–12

5 *Bernard Maybeck*
First Church of Christ Scientist,
Berkeley, Cal. 1910–12

on the East Coast, and the building of the Spanish missionaries in Southern California – but also the ideas and buildings which occurred in Europe during the nineteenth century. For Maybeck had been educated at the Ecole des Beaux Arts in Paris. The imprint of those years was not easily lost, nor did many of the notions acquired in Europe seem inappropriate to the tasks which needed to be faced in the Bay Region at the start of the century.

Maybeck is best remembered for his First Church of Christ Scientist (1910–12) on the corner of an urban plot on the edge of the central area of Berkeley. It is a low building lost among vegetation. The first impression is not of an enclosed volume but of an open pergola of dark redwood rails supported on concrete brackets and columns. The interior is an elaborate construction in concrete entirely Gothic in spirit. The lighting is subdued; there are occasional touches of colour but the concrete pillars and vaulting are left in their natural grey state. It is an ecclesiastical space which, one feels, could not have been uninfluenced by the writings of Pugin and the polemics on structure by Viollet-le-Duc. The exterior of the church combines two products created for quite a different market but both noteworthy for their ordinariness: large square asbestos tiles hung on the diagonal and factory windows imported from England. Clearly the building is a statement about certain propositions relating to architecture which have roots which, whether highly conscious or submerged, are historically traceable, and it expresses those propositions in a combination of old and novel forms, or, more, correctly, by the use of known elements in new situations. Yet the dominant and certainly immediate impression on any observer, whether Sunday worshipper, architectural pilgrim or visiting tourist, is not of intellectual propositions but of visual experiences understood largely emotionally. Such an impact is of course not unique to the Christian Science Church in Berkeley but is in fact the most common form of experiencing architecture. The fact is obvious but needs restatement.

It was in the latter part of 1955, a little over a year before his death in 1957 at the age of 95, that I met Maybeck. He sat in his deck chair among the dappled light below the eucalyptus trees on a terrace outside his house in the Berkeley hills. He looked frail but alert, happy to talk of his past as well as to listen about ideas now on the drawing board. He wore a pink crocheted beret to protect his head and one felt it probably carried nostalgic references to his days in France. We talked of Rome and St Peter's, which he remembered before Mussolini had cleared and vandalised its approaches, of his student days in the ateliers of the Beaux Arts in Paris, of Viollet-le-Duc, and briefly of his meeting with Frank Lloyd Wright.

The talk somehow veered much more towards Europe than towards his own work in Northern California. It may have been my presence yet clearly the experience had been important to him, and was probably most obvious in the Palace of Fine Arts in San Francisco which was like a brilliant Prix de Rome project that had actually been built.

He had at his feet a rough model of a church. It was a series of cutouts in hardboard of Gothic profiles which defined a nave and aisles. I was astonished to see what looked so very much like work in progress. I therefore turned to him and asked whether this is what he was now designing. Maybeck looked up from the model and replied: 'I never design buildings, I only study them.'

It seemed to me at the time that this simple statement, made casually during a leisurely conversation, typified a number of dilemmas in architectural thinking. Nor have the thirty-six years that have elapsed altered my impression of it as an indication of the problems that underlie so many architectural discussions, so many educational policies and so much architectural criticism. And through these of course affecting directly the built product.

The statement was probably an echo of Maybeck's earlier thoughts and interests. It is known from an announcement which appeared at the time that in 1891 Maybeck intended to translate Gottfried Semper's *Der Stil*. Two volumes had appeared in 1860 and 1863 as part of Semper's monumental attempt to trace the roots of architecture in the crafts and to establish its laws. It was a task which he never completed, and which perhaps in any case it was not possible to conclude satisfactorily.

Gottfried Semper (1803–79) had, significantly, studied law and mathematics before turning to architecture. He initially worked in Dresden until he found himself on the losing side in the revolutionary

6 *Bernard Maybeck*
Palace of Fine Arts, San Francisco,
Cal. 1915

11

7 Gottfried Semper
Design for the Canadian Section,
1851 Exhibition, London

movement of 1848. He fled in 1849 in the company of Richard Wagner and first moved to Paris. In 1850 he came to London, where he designed four of the national exhibits at the Great Exhibition of 1851 at the Crystal Palace and gave a number of lectures. During the course of one of these in 1853 he produced the following formula explaining architecture:

$$Y = F(x, y, z \ldots)$$

where Y = end result

x, y, z = different agents, forces which act together or separately and which are modified by the coefficient F

Though Semper does not define the variables in his equation and is in fact careful to leave the impact of these on each other open, he is nevertheless looking for a rational, scientific explanation for the differences between buildings. By extension, presumably such an understanding would also have its application when considering new buildings; it would be an educational tool. Semper does not appear to have lost his belief in such a scientific foundation throughout his years of teaching and building in Zürich, for in a passage in *Der Stil* which he emphasises typographically he again writes: 'Die Kunst . . . sie muss sich in den Prinzipien formaler Gestaltung genau nach den Gesetzen der Natur richten.' (In art . . . the formal design principles must direct themselves precisely to the laws of nature.)

It seems to me that when Maybeck asserted that he did not design, he was making a statement in the spirit of Semper's search for some analogue between architecture and science. To design had the connotations of an unscientific, perhaps intuitive pursuit; to study buildings implied to him a more serious, conceivably rational activity. Whether there is any validity to such an assumption is another matter and at this stage unimportant. What is significant, however, is that Maybeck clearly saw the distinction and that many architects of his time and after thought it critical to an intellectual understanding of architecture and vital as an educational assumption, even if they were not able to operate on the basis of such a notion as practising architects. Though the idea might not be immediately attainable it remained, like so many others, a mythological goal; and such myths are often more powerful than reality. If the basic attributes of a hypothesis, however, after critical examination and many attempts to put them into use, are not applicable, then to change the original hypothesis for an alternative version seems a desirable and necessary step rather than to continue to hope that some day the facts will fit.

The design/study dichotomy raises a further problem which is crucial and ought to be pointed out at the outset of any discussion of architecture – though, once stated, it may appear obvious. The word 'study' suggests an activity related to thinking, and thinking has immediate connections in most instances with language; it has in fact been described as 'talking with concealed musculature'. Language, whether of words or other symbols such as numbers, has a clearly dominant role in our culture. It is likely that both behaviourists and structuralists, for instance, would agree that it may even be one of our most characteristic attributes, without necessarily being in accord as to its origins. Skinner would consider it critical; Chomsky would certainly give it primacy; so would Lévi-Strauss. Edmund Leach, discussing the anthropological work of Lévi-Strauss, writes that his starting point was 'that the specifically human quality of human beings is that they have a language. At one level this allows man to communicate and form social relations and at another it is an essential element in the mysterious process we call "thinking", in that we must first categorise our environment and then represent these categories by symbols ("elements of language", "words") before we can "think" about them'.

The activity of *designing*, however, does not quite follow such a pattern. Although we may speak of a 'language of architecture', and it is recognised that the elements of architecture may have symbolic meanings (it would be difficult to imagine that they were devoid of these), nevertheless when I consider a building – its spatial relationships, its visual form, its finishes, its distribution of light – when in other words I go through some of the processes of designing, I attempt to *visualise* these forms and their attributes not as symbols but as realities. I do not at this stage use symbols which signify these spaces in the sense in which words signify things. It is only after this process has occurred that an architect will

8 Alvar Aalto
Sketch for Cultural Centre, Siena,
1966

draw or make scale models in order to test, elaborate and eventually communicate his architectural thoughts. 'Thinking' and 'communication' are thus not nearly as closely related as in verbal language.

This is a dilemma which Lévi-Strauss recognises in the case of music but which he characteristically dismisses rather grandly by making 'the creator of music a being like the gods'. Neither the problem nor the simile are of course new. Both are embodied in the myth of Pygmalion described by Ovid and both are behind the injunction against the making of images of persons and animals which prevailed in many areas of the Islamic world. The prohibition was not primarily based on the usual form of iconoclasm which forbids the worship of images but, perhaps more significantly, arose from the belief that the creation of such images in some way usurped the functions of God.

I do not in any way wish to claim such a divine status for the architect but only to emphasise that the first, critical and essential stages of architectural thinking must take the form of non-verbal thinking; that in fact it is extremely unlikely that Maybeck could have been studying a building using verbal thought processes in the accepted sense. It is a distinction which is crucial and which needs recognition if much confusion is to be avoided.

2

The desire to find some justification for design decisions which lies behind Semper's formula and writings and Maybeck's brief sentence was not a peculiarly nineteenth century phenomenon. It had existed for a very long time. Its characteristic form during the Renaissance was either a reference to nature as the original source or to the antique as the pure prototype. Both are in a sense variants of the Platonic teaching that perfection resides in the original, that there was once a perfect Form or Idea which has been progressively lost as subsequent developments tended to depart from that original. Only by going back to the perfect source of nature and the old is there therefore a chance, in the case of architecture, to at least stem the process of descent from the ideal.

The antique and nature were in any case already inextricably mixed up. Vitruvius, that somewhat self-justifying Augustan architect-writer, continually makes reference to nature as providing the guidelines to architectural correctness. In the case of the 'fundamental principles of architecture', for example:

'Symmetry is the proper agreement between members of the work itself, and the relation between the different parts and the whole general scheme, in accordance with a certain part selected as standard. Thus in the human body there is a kind of symmetrical harmony between forearm, foot, palm, finger and other small parts; and so it is with perfect buildings.'

and again

'Propriety is that perfection of style which comes when a work is authoritatively constructed on approved principles. It arises from prescription, from usage, or from nature.'

Because it is difficult to imagine and justify a source which is more basic than nature – whether expressed in abstract mathematical terms or more literally in formal analogies – it is seen as the ultimate arbiter, or as Alberti saw it in the fifteenth century: '. . . natura optima e divina maestra di tutte le cose' (nature is the best and divine teacher of all things).

9 *Francesco di Giorgio Studies in proportion; pag Turin Codex*

The most profound search for a rational explanation of the basis of architecure which preoccupied so much of the Renaissance tried to establish a correspondence between musical ratios and the proportions of buildings. The analysis of music was viewed as a mathematical science. Musical harmonies were part of nature and were therefore based on laws which were divinely ordained. Alberti, Palladio, Scamozzi, Vignola and others all thought that if buildings were based on these musical ratios not only would they be beautiful but, much more to the point, they would be correct, they would acquire a certainty.

The particular part of nature which is thought to be the appropriate model for architecture is of course a historically changing idea. Palladio, writing in 1570 in an age increasingly fascinated by the nature of the physical world, says in the preface to the fourth of his *Quattro Libri dell'Architettura*:

'If we consider the beautiful machine of the world, with how many wonderful ornaments it is filled, and how the heavens, by their continual revolutions, change the seasons according as nature requires, and their motion preserves itself by the sweetest harmony of temperature; we cannot doubt, but that the little temples we make, ought to resemble this very great one, which by His immense goodness, was perfectly completed with one word of His.'

Vitruvius, however, also had an Aristotelian view of progress, namely that there was an ascending principle at work in which the present embodied the highest developments. This was equally the view of most nineteenth century writers and architects. But as in the case of Vitruvius their belief in the present demanded a full historical knowledge of origins and of subsequent developments in order to acquire a proper understanding of the nature of the activity. Optimism demanded that the present was the highest achievement; uncertainty suggested that justification from the natural or archaic made challenge more difficult. Such a view would have been shared by Semper.

Semper delivered his London lectures, which embodied the bulk of what he was to elaborate in later years, before Darwin had published *The Origin of Species* in 1859. Most of Semper's allusions to science, and especially to the biological sciences and evolutionary ideas, were therefore pre-Darwinian and depended largely on the earlier writings of Cuvier. From these Semper had tried to establish some correspondence between the evolution of species and the existence of building types.

However, as I think the quotations from the London lecture of 1853 and *Der Stil* show, the intention went beyond any detailed analogy between some part of science and architecture, to a more general proposition that architecture was also subject to a series of scientific laws. What mattered therefore was to expend sufficient energy and scholarship in order to discover these. This particular belief, it could be argued, was just one more example of the widely held nineteenth century attitude that the then assumed methods of the sciences could be applied generally, or at least over a much wider range of topics than had previously been the case. This was after all central to Marx's writings, for instance, and although the suggestion is in dispute there is some evidence that Marx had hoped to dedicate the second volume of *Das Kapital* to Darwin, an honour which was declined in carefully ambiguous terms.

Semper's energy and scholarship were devoted to tracing the early history of weaving, pottery, carpentry and masonry, which he held to be the originators of architecture. Others before him – notably Laugier – had made similar excursions into the past in order to find the essential primitive hut as the source of all subsequent building, an 'Adam's house in paradise'. There was perhaps also a political bias to Semper's notion since he had been on the populist side in 1848. One suspects that he would have thought it only right and proper if architecture, which was now in the service of the ruling classes, had had its roots in a folk culture. But dominantly, as in biology, the search for origins was a search for laws; architecture ought to have these too. And the eventual intellectual and indeed practical aim in terms of building was to be able to formulate from these laws a 'true style'.

Now let us suppose for the moment that Semper was right and that there is a general correspondence between architecture and evolutionary theory. The greater explanatory power of Darwin's work and of the post-Darwinian period in general ought merely to provide further insights into architecture. Yet if we take a key assumption from evolutionary theory, such as that the creation of new species derives from chance mutations, then by corollary the emergence of a number of new styles at any time should simply give hope that some of these will survive and continue to flourish. Eclecticism in architecture ought thus to be looked at from the evolutionary point of view with optimisim. However, this is not at all what Semper or most of his contemporaries had in mind.

10 *Charles Eisen 'Allegory of Architecture Returning to its Natural Model' frontispiece to 'Essai sur l'architecture' by M. A. Laugier, second edition, 1755*

The 'Battle of the Styles', that is between Gothic and Classical in particular, was to be settled ideally by some reference to a higher authority such as science, and certainly was not to degenerate into diffuse guerilla skirmishes between innumerable eclectics.

As a practising architect involved in day-to-day decisions on how to design, say, the Art Gallery in Dresden, the ETH in Zurich or the town hall in Winterthur, Semper was a middling neo-classicist with Florentine preferences. Yet in a discussion of the products shown at the 1851 Exhibition he attacked the prevalence of stylistic copying. If again we assume some analogy with evolutionary theory, it has to be pointed out that one of the essential attributes of any living organism is its invariance; a species will survive only if it can copy itself. Without such successful reproduction of itself it would simply cease to exist.

The ability of a style to withstand copying may indeed be one of its strengths, and be necessary for its survival. It might almost be said that unless it is copied it does not constitute a style in the accepted sense of the word; we are simply dealing with a 'rogue' manifestation. The fact that Semper was using a stylistic vocabulary which had been modified for over two thousand years was itself a testimony to its usefulness and thus its survival value. In this detailed instance an analogy between architecture and biology may thus turn out to be valid, though not

11 Gotfried Semper
Art gallery, Dresden, 1847–54

19

in the way intended by Semper. The point, however, is not whether there is a valid analogy between biology or any other science and architecture, but that the search for such analogues or models only confuses the argument. First, it attempts equivalences between unlike things – between, say, buildings and animals not at the level of symbols (as in a possible analysis in structuralist anthropology, for example) but in their parallel historical development. More important, it confuses the findings of a particular science with the idea of a scientific method.

The question whether a scientific method, used in its most general sense, can be applied to architecture depends, in the first instance, on whether there is a scientific content within the built environment and whether there is a method which is sufficiently wide to embrace such a possible fringe discipline. The suggestion I wish to make is that there is such a method, that it is extremely general, and that it has very serious and fruitful implications for many aspects of architecture, including those in which the scientific content may be slight. Moreover the consequences which stem from it are, I believe, of value well outside the realm of science. It depends on that view of science which has been elaborated in the writings of Karl Popper, starting with the *Logik der Forschung* published in Vienna in 1934; this appeared in English as *The Logic of Scientific Discovery* in 1959, and was subsequently both expanded and summarised in *Objective Knowledge: an Evolutionary Approach* which first came out in 1972. Popper has also applied some of the basic attitudes which originated from an understanding of the philosophy of science to a discussion of history in *The Open Society and its Enemies* (1945/1966) and *The Poverty of Historicism* (1957), and I am therefore encouraged to believe that an extension of some of these ideas to architecture may not be entirely impossible or inappropriate.

The attempt is, in my view, well worth making. The intellectual underpinning of architectural criticism has at present hardly any arguable assumptions; or at any rate where these are supposed to exist they appear to me to be extremely narrow and to offer highly limited answers to small problems. But perhaps most important of all, the attempt would seem to be worth making because of the frequent dissatisfaction with the products of current architectural thinking. Modern architecture is, rightly or wrongly, unpalatable to many of its consumers (or at least so it is said and frequently believed), is blamed for the destruction of what has been carefully established in many cities over the centuries, and is only weakly, if at all, defended by its practitioners. I take this to be a sufficiently important problem of general interest, and an adequate starting point for any discussion of architectural questions.

Let us first, however, return to Semper and then to Popper.

3

In 1871 Semper moved to Vienna, which was already then that highly cosmopolitan but paradoxical capital of the Austro-Hungarian empire. It was experiencing a great increase in wealth and a rapid rise in population – from 476 220 in 1857 to 2 031 420 in 1910 – and the city limits were being extended at the same time as the Emperor Francis Joseph was rebuilding large portions of the centre and particularly the great Ringstrasse. It was one of the prestigious projects of the imperial reconstruction with which Semper was to be concerned. He designed with Carl von Hasenauer the new Kunsthistorische Museum (1872–89) to house the applied arts in which he had been interested for so long. His main concern, however, judging by his writings, was not for their visual attributes but for their didactic implications, and he had already elaborated a plan for an 'Ideal Museum' as a teaching instrument during his stay in London twenty years earlier. Gottfried Semper died in Vienna in 1876 before the museum was complete.

The next generation of Viennese appears to have reacted against the wealth accumulated by its fathers and to have taken up intellectual and artistic causes with a single-mindedness which was remarkable and which had quite astonishing results. Hapsburg

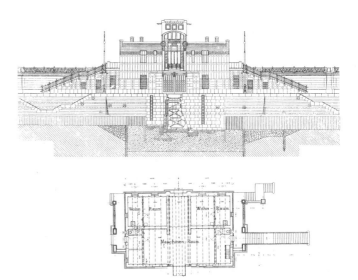

12 Otto Wagner
Sluice gate and control building,
Kaiserbad Dam, Vienna, 1904–8

13 Otto Wagner
*Staircase and lift shaft, Linke
Wienzeile 40 (Majolica House),
Vienna, 1898–9*

Vienna had in its intellectual circles in the two or
three decades before the crash of 1918 the muscians
Gustav Mahler, Arnold Schoenberg, Richard Strauss;
the painters Gustav Klimt, Egon Schiele, Oskar
Kokoschka; the architects Otto Wagner and Adolf
Loos; the Secession architects Joseph Olbrich and
Josef Hoffmann; the founders of psychoanalysis
Sigmund Freud and Viktor Adler as well as Carl Jung;
the scientist and philosopher Ernst Mach and the
young philosopher Ludwig Wittgenstein; the writers
Rainer Maria Rilke and Hugo von Hofmannstahl; to
select only those names which have remained best
known, especially abroad. It excludes, for instance,
highly influential writers who have not become
familiar outside German-speaking countries simply
because of language problems.

It must also be said that it bred such politicians as
Georg von Schönerer and Karl Lueger, who largely
initiated the ideas of a Pan-German National Social-
ism which were eventually to be taken up by Adolf
Hitler. Before ever absorbing these political notions
Hitler was totally entranced by the architecture and
life of the Ringstrasse on his first visit to Vienna.

The architects Wagner and Loos were both
influenced by Gottfried Semper and both were to
make their impact on subsequent architectural
developments. This was particularly true of Loos and
two of his designs; a house built in 1910 and a block
near the Hofburg of the same year which was to
become the occasion of a legal battle on account of its

14 Adolf Loos
*Building on Michaelerplatz, Vienna,
1910–11*

15 *Adolf Loos*
Kärtner Bar, Vienna, 1907

apparent public offensiveness. Loos is best known and most often quoted because of his essay 'Ornament and Crime', a passionate moral and economic outcry against the excesses of ornamentation. Ornament might just be acceptable if genuinely, organically, related to the cultural life of its time. Who was to decide what was and what was not organic in its relation, however, was not spelled out. The main objection to ornament was grounded in an evolutionary theory of Loos' devising and the fact that criminals and degenerate aristocrats were frequently tattooed. He was thus moved to announce: 'I have discovered the following truth and present it to the world: *cultural evolution is equivalent to the removal of ornament from articles of daily use*'.

Somewhat as in the case of Semper, though, the relation between the written statement of prescription or intent – 'we have conquered ornament, we have won through to lack of ornamentation

24

. . . . Lack of ornament is a sign of spiritual strength'
– and the executed architectural statement could
assume a number of interpretations. This is really not
surprising since architecture does not readily lend
itself to simple equivalences between verbal definitions and built form. It ought in any case to be
recognised that Loos was against *applied* decoration
and not against the decorative qualities inherent in
materials such as marble. He also had, on his own
admission, a very considerable admiration for the
rigorous attributes of neo-classicism.

A glance at the garden elevation of the Loos house
of 1910 will immediately reveal that the break with
the past was not as drastic as it might seem. The
building is a balanced symmetrical composition as of
a small palazzo or Schloss; the windows change
proportions on each of the three floors in much the
same way as in a palazzo, so that the narrow
openings on the top floor and the small square
openings above them suggest entablature and cor-
nice; the terrace and steps are those of a small
château . . . . A very similar kind of analysis can
obviously be made of the building on the Michaelerplatz. An immediately visible use of material as
decoration in his shops or the Josephine Baker house
can hardly be denied.

Loos was later to have an influence on the Bauhaus
and through that remarkable school on the whole of
modern architecture. He was also, both as an
architect and as a writer with an incisive moral

25

17 *Ludwig Wittgenstein*
Stonborough-Wittgenstein House,
Vienna, 1928

standpoint searching for an essential and simple truth, to have his effect on Wittgenstein. Ludwig Wittgenstein was trained as an engineer before he became a philosopher, and in the curious intermissions between his two philosophical works he designed a house for his sister in Vienna which had many affinities with the work of Loos. In its general form and especially in its meticulous detailing it reduces architectural elements to a quite remarkable level of simplicity. Or as Wittgenstein put it in a letter of appreciation to the firm responsible for the ironmongery: 'I can say that it would have been impossible without your work to erect the building with the precision and objectivity necessary for this kind of construction.'

It was into the final period of this milieu, soon to suffer the defeat of 1918 and the disastrous influenza epidemic which followed almost immediately, that Karl Popper was born in 1902. His parents were members of that prosperous and thoughtful middle class which formed the influential but not the ruling circles of Vienna. Politically his early leanings were towards Marxism and he was later to become a supporter of the Social Democrats; he did social work under Adler and at one stage felt such a need for identification with the working class that he apprenticed himself to a carpenter; he was extremely interested in music and the society of Private Concerts founded by Schoenberg, and at the end of his studies became a schoolteacher of mathematics and physics.

When he turned to philosophy, which in the Viennese intellectual society of that day was not an esoteric topic but a subject that was seen to have relevance to everyday matters, he found himself out of sympathy with the currently established views and to some extent even the accepted notion of what constituted the important philosophical problems. Many of these revolved around the relation between 'reality' and 'language' and the need to define the essentials of language in much the same way that Loos was anxious to strip architecture to its essentials. Otto Neurath, the social scientist who founded the Ernst Mach Verein which was the forerunner of the Vienna Circle (the Wiener Kreis of the logical positivists), was said to have labelled Popper as 'the official opposition'. Popper is certainly extremely

26

opposed to the whole argument of Wittgenstein's *Tractatus Logico Philosophicus*, which has in the last few years been recognised, despite its relation to the work of Bertrand Russell, as a philosophical work very much of its time and place. Its attempt to define the boundaries between 'sense' and 'nonsense' and its equation of such 'sense' with 'the totality of true propositions of the totality of the natural sciences' was part of the general movement which tried to unmask sham, especially in the arts. Popper reserves his approval for Wittgenstein's conclusions: the 'consequence of his doctrine is recognised by Wittgenstein himself, for he writes: "My propositions are elucidatory in this way: he who understands me finally recognises them as senseless . . . ". The result is important. Wittgenstein's own philosophy is senseless and is admitted to be so'. The whole attempt is misguided because 'it is meaningless to speak about a correspondence between a statement and a fact'. But this is a problem to which I shall return in so far as it affects the discussion of architecture; certainly most of science manages quite well without being too concerned by this worry.

Popper was to develop a great many of his most significant ideas in the philosophy of science, and through these in philosophy in general, from a consideration of three topics in which he was particularly interested and which were also the subject of debate in the Vienna of the 1920s: Marxism, Freudian psychoanalysis and Einstein's Theory of Relativity. All three made claims to be scientific. Yet any serious look at these three explanations of quite different phenomena also revealed their quite different approaches to providing explanations and accepting criticism. Psychoanalytical theory and Marxism tried to provide extremely wide-ranging explanations of personal behaviour and of history which took on all the characteristics of dogma, of a religious faith revealed to the initiated and always able to counter arguments by pitying or accusing the opponent of not yet having reached the stage of full understanding. Opposition could thus always be said to be due not to any cogency of the argument but to some notion which formed part of the theory itself.

It was thus possible to say that any disbelief in the importance of infantile sexuality, for instance, was itself due to a guilt complex developed from the practices of infantile sexuality. Similarly, the suggestion that Marx's forecasts based on a particular understanding of history might not be the only or valid interpretation could be countered with the statement that non-Marxist versions of history have been modified by the ruling class in its own interest and are thus to be discounted. This is not to suggest that any of these and a great many other aspects may not have their effect on our understanding, but only that this kind of argument fails to allow for any form of discussion by which these theories could be tested; there does not appear to be a possible corroboration of the existence of the Id, for instance.

Where testable propositions were forecast by Marx, for example, some of the most important of these have not occurred: the full capitalist stage of development was not reached in any present-day communist country prior to revolution, nor were all of these revolutions based on an industrial proletariat as demanded by the theory; nor has the polarisation of classes into an owning capitalist group on the one hand and a powerless working class on the other happened, but intermediary groups have arisen as suggested in James Burnham's analysis in *The Managerial Society*. Though theory and events do not tally, the theory continues to be propagated by Marxists as a scientific explanation of history. So does psychoanalytical theory as an explanation of the workings of our unconscious and subconscious.

The discrepancy between theory and events does not necessarily devalue the contribution made by Marx, whose humanitarian instincts and concern for the alienation of the worker have greatly affected the attitude towards labour in almost every country of the world. In any case, many of the exaggerated claims for the theory were made by Marxists rather than by Marx himself. His work moreover contains many contradictions between the early and late writings, and *Das Kapital* was unfinished at the time of his death. The gap between forecast and subsequent happenings only diminishes the claim of the theory to be correct and thus, within its own terms, scientific. Very much the same is true of the work of Sigmund Freud, who has clearly enormously enlarged our interest in the workings of the human personality and has affected our view on education, on criminology and on art, to select only a few topics, and made us reconsider many of our moral values. Such an achievement need not, however, inevitably belong to the realm of science.

Einstein's formulation of his Theory of Relativity was put forward in a significantly different way; it actually proposed a test by which it could be refuted. It was crucial to the theory that light should be subject to gravitational pull and that the light from a star would thus be deflected by the sun, for instance.

'Normally we cannot see such stars, because of the sun's brilliance, but if we could, the deflection of their light rays would make them appear to be in a different position from those we know them to occupy. And the predicted difference could be checked by photographing a fixed star in such circumstances by day, and then again at night when the sun was not there. Eddington tested this by one of the most famous scientific observations of the century. In 1919 he led an expedition to a point in Africa from which, he calculated, a forthcoming eclipse of the sun was about to render such a star visible, and hence photographable by day. On 29th May the observations were made. And they corroborated Einstein's theory.'

Taking the example set by Einstein's formulations and looking at the history of scientific theories, Popper argued that one of the hallmarks of any scientific theory was that it put itself continually at risk. It was always open to challenge, to refutation and to the likelihood of being superseded by a new and more powerful theory, by an explanation which either showed the earlier version to be wrong or included the earlier form in a wider, more revealing theory, one with a greater content. If, therefore, there was to be some line of demarcation between science and non-science the line should be drawn so that only that which could be tested and was potentially refutable should be called scientific. In terms of 'sense' and 'nonsense' in Wittgenstein's argument, science was always potentially 'non-sense'. Any suggestion that the true should be equated with the scientific was therefore completely misguided. It is no wonder that holding such views Popper was regarded as a member of the intellectual opposition. Nor have these uncomfortable views really become the conventional wisdom since those early days in Vienna, though they are now often accepted if not always acted upon; they place a heavy responsibility on criticism and discussion rather than on revealed wisdom, which may not make for immediate popular appeal.

It ought to be said straight away that any such line of demarcation in no way implies that statements which belong to one side are valuable and those which belong to the other are not. Popper is simply making an operational distinction between science and non-science and not a value judgement. He again differs here from both Ernst Mach and Wittgenstein who thought the non-scientific, the metaphysical, to be valueless. There is no such implication anywhere in his writings. Though Popper's enthusiasm for science as a manifestation of human culture is enormous and unabated, the values which he sees as crucial may arise out of science but ultimately lie elsewhere: 'Man has created new worlds – of language, of music, of poetry, of science; and the most important of these is the world of moral demands, for equality, for freedom, and for helping the weak.'

4

If the position of the line of demarcation first worked out by Popper in the winter of 1919–20 but published a good deal later is accepted – and I know of no other which is equally useful or which comes closer to what one knows about the scientific method – then it may be possible to look at the question whether or not architecture has a relation to science in terms of this particular formulation. The problems which are implied by the design/study dichotomy may come closer to being resolved or perhaps cease to be seen as problems.

It seems to me that it may be possible to isolate certain elements within architecture and, having done so, to assume that these are falsifiable. The function of the structure of a building, for example, must be primarily that of support, to counteract gravity. Structure is calculated on the basis of certain theories in statics, the strength of materials, the behaviour of materials over time and so on. If when completed it does not stand up, this could be said to refute the structural theories on which it was based (assuming the absence of errors in calculation, proper workmanship etc., factors which are usually included in pragmatically devised safety factors). This kind of assumption is also embodied in the accepted methods for laboratory testing of structural members or structural models in the sense that a beam, for instance, is not normally tested for its ability to carry a previously determined superimposed load, but is gradually loaded until it fails. The whole example is of course a rather obvious one, and it could be argued that it does not properly belong to architecture but to engineering or physics. Yet it should be remembered that structure plays a very important role in architecture, both in individual buildings and historically, and that there are a good many descriptions of architecture from the primitive hut onwards which put very considerable emphasis on structural developments and see them as perhaps the main determinants of architectural form. This is perhaps not surprising since structure can be thought of as the basic element without which no building can exist; it is the last part to which architecture can be reduced and still remain a recognisable entity. There have

18 *North Portico, Erechtheion, Acropolis, Athens, 420–406 BC*

clearly been periods when structure and structural ingenuity appear to have done a great deal to shape buildings in a particular way, and this seems perhaps even stronger in retrospect when we have forgotten the other considerations which were crucial at the time. It is impossible to consider the great Gothic cathedral building period without recognising the structural ingenuity of the Master Masons. It could also be argued that Gothic had a successful revival in the nineteenth century precisely because structural principles had been evolved and building materials developed which allowed the construction of Gothic spaces with comparative ease; this in fact allowed the completion of cathedrals such as that at Cologne, started in the middle of the thirteenth century.

It would be hard to think of this as the whole story, however. When Frank Lloyd Wright stood under the dramatic cantilever of the balcony over the brook at Bear Run as the shuttering was being struck, he was putting his life at risk for a number of reasons. Primarily of course it was because he was that kind of personality. But also he was convinced that the calculations and the construction in reinforced concrete could not be 'falsified' by the removal of the temporary supports. His interest in that form of construction stemmed in the first instance, however, from the belief that the visual effect produced by the cantilever was vital to the success of his architectural concept. The structural solution and the ambition to push it to its limits arose from a desire for a particular visual form and no other.

Structure is not the only element capable of being isolated. We construct criteria of utility, for instance, in order to distinguish between buildings which are acceptable and those which are not. Most statistical analyses of housing, to take perhaps the best-known example, would list dwellings without inside lavatories, with only shared cooking facilities, without heating or other similar essential facilities by the standards of the country concerned, in order to arrive at the total number of unfit dwellings which ought to be demolished or renovated. The unfit dwellings in a sense refuted the criteria, which in turn were based on more general social theories about acceptable standards, the need to provide a level of housing as a matter of social policy, the social and personal damage casued by inadequate housing provision, or an even more general attitude to the problems of social equality.

Although the method has some similarity to that which may be said to have applied in the case of structure, it really starts in the last resort from arbitrary criteria rather than a scientific hypothesis. This is the case largely because the social theories from which the criteria are derived are in themselves not formulated in such a way as to be falsifiable: they are not scientific in terms of Popper's line of demarcation. What the example does show, however, is that we often proceed from a standpoint where we identify the faults and then attempt to correct these, rather than by specifying the allegedly correct. We may not know what the cooking facilities should be, but we believe that if they are shared, social difficulties arise; similarly we may not be able to specify the form of heating most suitable, but we know that the absence of heating is injurious to health in cold climates. It is a general point to which Popper returns again and again, especially in *The Open Society and its Enemies*, and it has, I propose to argue, considerable relevance to architectural design and urban planning well beyond the range of the two certainly trivial examples I have just cited.

It is also possible to imagine that buildings might be refuted as objects with a defined purpose in a somewhat different and perhaps more widespread way. The assumption might be that buildings are like ordinary artefacts made for a prescribed use and that if they do not fulfil that purpose they have simply failed. If a knife were to be produced which could not cut, we would discard it as useless; we would not really accept it as a knife. In this sense it should be possible to ascribe specific uses to buildings and then to test whether the completed buildings are able to meet the requirements which arise from those particular use patterns. To take an extreme example, the purpose of a hospital, as an institution supported by its specific building, is to help those who are ill to become well. If, however, the circulation of septic waste has been designed in such a way as to cause cross-infection and patients acquire illnesses which they did not previously have, then the hospital design could be said to have failed a crucial test. Clearly it has in one respect, but in that respect only. Any possible falsification refers to an isolated element and not to the building as a whole.

Studies have been conducted which consist of follow-up analyses to see how buildings are performing in use, and especially to see whether the intentions of the designers are borne out by the way in which people behave within the buildings. Although glaring discrepancies may occur which reveal either a misunderstanding of the real needs by the architect, or a change in the assumed needs subsequent to design, or the construction of mistaken provisions on the basis of correct assumptions, none of the studies have been able to test all aspects of the architecture or to produce a convincing refutation of the building as a totality. No doubt this is partly due to the extreme difficulty of forecasting human behaviour and to the fact that buildings are not deterministic in their effect. Great efforts were made at one time to establish design criteria for housing layouts which would aid friendship formation, for

34

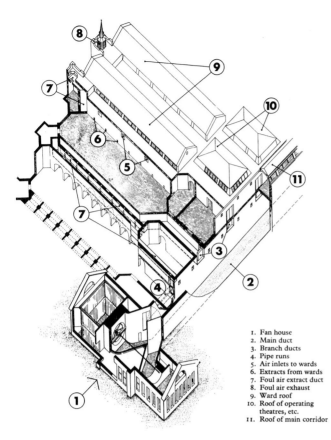

20 *Royal Victoria Hospital, Belfast,
1903*
*cutaway of complete ventilating
system*

1. Fan house
2. Main duct
3. Branch ducts
4. Pipe runs
5. Air inlets to wards
6. Extracts from wards
7. Foul air extract duct
8. Foul air exhaust
9. Ward roof
10. Roof of operating
    theatres, etc.
11. Roof of main corridor

instance, but none have yet been found which have any validity outside the particular situation in which they were investigated. Studies of vandalism may show a higher statistical correlation between certain kinds of spatial arrangements (absence of overlooking, failure to define the private from the public and thus help identify strangers etc.) and certain forms of violent behaviour, but these again refer to social groups at a particular time and in a particular place. In other words there is no evidence that specific physical conditions invariably evoke specific forms of behaviour.

Even quite detailed studies under controlled conditions, such as an investigation in a psychiatric ward in which the behaviour of patients before and after certain groupings of furniture had been re-arranged, did nothing to support architectural determinism. Not only was activity influenced outside the boundaries of the area under investigation but many of the changes which took place were not expected either in themselves or in the chain of effects which they set up. The users of the space falsified the hypothesis of the investigators as to how they would react under new conditions.

There is in any case a serious logical objection to the idea of determinism and to its extension as a basis for architectural design. In order to be certain that a design has any kind of correspondence to the activities which may occur within a building it would be necessary to list each and every one of the activities in every respect in which they might interact with the building. The probability of being able to do so is extremely low, and it is likely that if n activities were enumerated it would be possible to think of $n + 1$ activities. It would also be necessary to assume that not all criteria are equally important. Some form of relative weighting ought therefore to be applied to each activity in terms of its possible influence on the design. It is difficult to imagine that such weighting could ever be carried out objectively.

Any behaviouristic theory of architectural determinism is sure to be in a weak position on the available evidence, and is only likely to gain support because of the flattering importance which it ascribes to architecture and thus to architects. Architecture is at most 'probabilistic'. It can encourage certain kinds of activities within a given cultural context, suggest ways of behaviour, open up possibilities or curtail them, but it cannot determine the uses to which it should be put; there is no simple, fixed one-to-one relationship between space and activity.

Because it has been seen that the totality of a building may be difficult to specify in the sense of defining criteria which should be met, attempts have been made to take certain particular functions which in normal practice are related to definable zones within a building – for instance the activity of entering a house – and to establish for these performance specifications. These would take the form of listing the desirable attributes from the point of view of the user which such a zone should have in order to satisfy the functions which are performed in it. The most ambitious attempt along these lines was made by Christopher Alexander, Sarah Ishikawa and Murray Silverstein (1968) in *A Pattern Language which Generates Multi-Service Centers*. The work recognises

36

Text with pattern:

IF: Any space where more than 20 people are to meet for face to face discussion,

THEN:

1. *The meeting room contains concentric tiers of seats – the plan may be circular or square.*
2. *Seats in succeeding rows are staggered.*
3. *There is a fence, just above knee height, along each row of seats.*
4. *Each tier is ten inches above the one before it.*
5. *One corner in the top row is reserved for visual exhibits.*

A two tiered room will have a capacity of 36 (less circulation). A three tiered room will have a capacity of 72 (less circulation). A four tiered room will have a capacity of 120 (less circulation).

---

21 Page from 'A Pattern Language which generates Multi-Service Centers', by Christopher Alexander, Sara Ishikawa and Murray Silverstein, 1968

the difficulties which exist in any attempt to create an architectural prototype for a characteristic building and it therefore suggests the process of fragmenting the problem into its components.

'What we have devised then, is a system of generating principles, which can be richly transformed according to local circumstances but which never fail to convey their essentials. This is rather like a grammar. English grammar is a set of generating principles which generate all the possible sentences of English. It would be preposterous to suppose that one could convey the full richness of the English language by means of a few well-chosen "prototypical" sentences.'

The analogy is dangerous, however. Grammar may provide the rules for sentence structure, though as Chomsky and others have found these are extremely difficult to formulate, but it says nothing about the content of such sentences. It does not distinguish, to use the classic example, between 'the cat sat on the mat' and 'the mat sat on the cat', between sense and surrealism. This is particularly true in English since gender does not affect the definite article or word endings.

There is a further danger, which is probably even more relevant in applying the analogy to architecture. Strictly speaking, grammar is not a system of conventions which we devise in order to be able to construct intelligible sentences but an attempt to construct a model of the rules which already exist in the language as it is used. Most native speakers of a language are perfectly capable of communicating in it but may be profoundly ignorant of the rules which describe grammatical constructions. If the analogy were to hold, the claim would have to be made that in architecture there are also underlying structures which govern the combination of elements according to some discoverable rules. Alexander and his

22 Page from 'The Timeless Way of Building' by Christopher Alexander, 1979

colleagues made the opposite suggestion in 1968, namely that it is *they* who are devising 'a system of generating principles'.

There has been an important shift in the arguments which Christopher Alexander and his group have used since then and which are embodied in six books. The most significant change as far as the present discussion is concerned is that *The Pattern of Language* of 1977 not only tends to describe each of the patterns in prescriptive terms but frequently starts from a diagnosis of what appears to be a malfunction in that particular architectural element. The suggested pattern, in other words, tries to put right something which is obviously not working satisfactorily at present; often the assumption is that it did so in the past. The illustrations which are used in the book certainly suggest a feeling for a lost golden age. On the other hand Alexander's later *The Timeless Way of Building* (1979) does suggest that the 'the language, and the processes which stem from it, merely release the fundamental order which is native to us'; that the rules about space are like the rules about language. The most radical difference from the earlier statements can be found in what can be read as a case study of the method, *The Linz Cafe* (1981), to which I shall return later, and also in *The Production of Houses* (1985). The argument was modified virtually out of recognition in *A New Theory of Urban Design* (1987) since the rules were being set out by an authority for designers to follow.

In terms of actual design application the method suggested by the establishment of a pattern language may or may not be useful, but a number of problems inherent in it ought to be immediately recognised apart from those of analogy. The first is that there can be no certainty that all the necessary criteria and *only* those necessary have actually been listed, either singly or acting in a new manner in combination with each other. The number of these, allowing for the possible permutations between them, is also likely to be extremely large. If this objection is countered by saying that the listing would deal only with the important criteria, the next problem is who is to decide what is important, and much of the apparent virtue of the method – a kind of neutrality through an exhaustive scanning of the problem – is immediately lost. There is a further objection: if the performance specifications set numerical limits, upper or lower, for any one function and this process is then repeated for others, when these limitations are combined rigid results may occur. These are far less satisfactory, even within the given criteria, than if one or other of the limitations had been relaxed. For example, Lionel March has analysed a set of specifications for home layouts which Alexander put forward in *The City as a Mechanism for Sustaining Human Contact* and shown the rather needless difficulties which arise.

But to me the most serious objection stems from the supposition that verbal specification is able to communicate all the attributes which are thought to be desirable within an architectural space. As I have already suggested, the translation of any specification into design must at some stage take the form of non-verbal thinking and there can therefore be no logical assurance that all the aspects of the verbal statement correspond to the architectural fact. It is but one aspect of the general problem of correspondence theory. Conversely, if the specification is to be given in non-verbal form, in the form of a drawing for instance, then it is no longer only a statement of desirable criteria but a model of the solution. This is immediately obvious from the drawings which accompany certain examples of Alexander's patterns. The authors of the Building Bulletins first produced by the Ministry of Education in 1955 and then by the Department of Education and Science, for example, have become aware of how even the most tentative drawings of parts of schools tend to get translated into actual design because these are an answer to the problem and not its statement.

A somewhat different attempt to resolve some of these difficulties – including the desire for a more scientific method – might be ascribed to the building of mathematical models in town planning and architecture. Exaggerated claims have been made on their behalf, usually by those not responsible for their construction. It ought therefore to be clearly recognised that such a model is always only a partial representation of reality, that if it were not 'unfaithful' the model would be reality itself and not a representation. The model is in any case constructed by using selected existing data in order to understand their relationships and to study the effect of manipulating certain of the variables. For instance,

Slope the roof or make a vault of it, make its entire surface visible, and bring the eaves of the roof down low, as low as 6'0" or 6'6" at places like the entrance, where people pause. Build the top storey of each wing right into the roof, so that the roof does not only cover it, but actually surrounds it.

23 Page from 'A Pattern Language' by Christopher Alexander, Sara Ishikawa and Murray Silverstein, 1977

the early and now classic Lowry model allocates residents about workplaces and services about residents; these services in turn generate more residents and the model is iterated until equilibrium is reached. Echenique has adapted and improved this basic formulation by taking into account the physical infrastructure of a town, i.e. the stock of land, building and roads. Nor is this the end of the process of improvement; clearly the number of relationships which could be considered is capable of being increased. Nevertheless, though mathematical models may now be regarded as the most effective way of describing the mass of relationships that exist in an urban system they do not themselves explain those relationships. Models may be constructed on the basis of some hypothesis which attempts such an explanation, and the degree of correlation between the hypothesis and a model using existing data may therefore be a test of such a hypothesis. If the same hypothesis is then used to develop a new design, that design can only be tested in the model on the assumption that the relationships which are being looked at would behave in much the same way as they do in the situations from which the data were derived. This inference is logically weak, and in any case the process omits those relationships which were not studied as such and the effects on them of those that were. We are again faced with the same difficulty of understanding the totality of the built form through another descriptive medium, irrespective of whether we consider one which already exists or one which is about to be created.

Any commonsense look at how buildings are actually used and appraised would, I propose, dispel most of these problems. We do not treat buildings as if they were ordinary artefacts, like a knife, in the much too simple way I first suggested. Even a casual survey of the existing stock of buildings in any city would show that houses are being used as offices, schools or workshops, that warehouses become studios, that palaces may be art galleries, that chapels are used as club rooms, that an urban open space can be a car park one day a week and a market on another or, as in Singapore, an open-air restaurant in the evening. One of the most famous art galleries in the world, the Uffizi in Florence, is still known by the name of its original function as an office; one of the most enticing hotels is a former palace on the lake at Udaipur in Rajasthan.

The idea of a typology of building forms, implied by the suggestion that specific purposes generate specific building arrangements, is of long standing but has been difficult to demonstrate so far in any satisfactory way. While it has been possible, for instance, to write *A History of Building Types*, such historical analysis has not been able to show how a given shape is the inevitable outcome of a known set of uses, nor as one turns the pages is it invariably obvious which building type is being illustrated, except when the contents of the building are clearly revealed. If, for example, one obscures the bookshelves on the picture of Labrouste's Bibliothèque Ste Geneviève of 1843–51 one can easily believe that one is looking at a nineteenth-century train shed or market hall. Conversely, if one looks at the concourse of Grand Central Station in New York one is meant to think of the Baths of Caracalla. The suitability of buildings to particular functions may depend a great deal on small or middle-scale adjustments within them. It thus makes implausible an architectural typology based on use. To assume that such a typology is possible is, I believe, to take too limited a view of what influences the making of a building.

It seems to me significant that when we look at the architecture of the past we rarely try to resolve this sort of problem. Our first question is unlikely to be whether or not Chartres was a successful church after

24 Henri Labrouste
Bibliothèque Ste. Geneviève, Paris,
1843–50

41

its consecration, or whether Shah Jahan found the Taj Mahal a suitable memorial for his queen. Nor even, faced with the outline of the Parthenon or the temple ruins of Polonnaruwa, do we ask whether their present state is the result of a structural collapse, of some miscalculation or other mishap which refuted their original assumptions. We simply do not view architecture in this way. The suggestions seem ludicrous and rightly so.

This is in no way to suggest that structural failure is an excusable event or that user studies may not serve extremely valuable purposes or that it is pointless to consider the assumed functions of a building when working on its design. None of these notions are in any way implied. I only want to draw attention to the limited range of problems which any particular 'study' of architecture is able to examine, and to point out that even the sum of such studies is unlikely to reveal the totality of architecture as it is used, sensed and understood in the everyday environment.

5

As was evident from the previous section, many of
the ideas which attempt to give architecture a
scientific basis, or at least some scientific support
(and at the same time try and bestow on it some
academic respectability), start from a belief in
behaviourism, namely that our activities can be
explained as being entirely the mechanical reactions
to sensory stimuli. Many of the sensory stimuli which
we receive are considerably influenced and often
even controlled by the built environment, so it is easy
to conclude that architecture will indeed determine
human activity. If it does so, then through design we
shall be able to mould the actions of the users of the
buildings. This has been an implied and often stated
assumption behind the architectural thinking of the
present century and has even enabled it to make
moral claims.

Such a view of the deterministic effect of architecture is of course only a special instance of a general
belief in the correctness of inductive reasoning, of the
belief that having observed certain patterns in the
past we can correctly forecast identical patterns of
activity under identical future conditions. That this is
an assumption we are not entitled to make, either in
architecture or in science, I shall return to later. That
it should ever have been made in the case of
architecture is not really surprising, however, in view
of its more recent antecedents.

Two ideas in common currency bolstered much of
the thinking behind many architectural and planning
concepts: the first was the set of utopian ideals which
emerged during the industrial revolution, largely as a
result of it; the second was the frequent – and mostly
facile – analogy with engineering which was under-
standably made in a period of rapid technological
development.

The ideal city is, of course, a long-standing dream,
the creation of a kind of paradise, of a Celestial City,
on earth. Only rarely did the dream become any kind
of reality, even though the word paradise comes from
the Old Persian for garden and the vision therefore
often had some physical embodiment. The atrium or
porticoed garden court, for instance, 'of the early
Christian basilica was often called *paradisus'*. By the

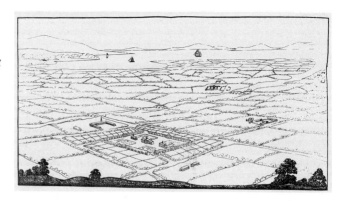

25 Robert Owen, 1817
'Village of Harmony and
Cooperation'
a settlement for 1200 people covering
500 hectares

late eighteenth and early nineteenth century utopian ideals began to be turned into small-scale but practical experiments. The ideals of Robert Owen, of Charles Fourier, of Etienne Cabet, of the religious groups in North America such as the Shakers were first and dominantly social and political. But because they were utopian they presupposed a serious restructuring of society, which invariably demanded parallel changes in the built environment. These more often involved new or at least amended architectural organisations rather than innovations in appearance. The feeling of a need to make stylistic changes came later. What was important to subsequent thinking, however, was the fact that the creation of utopian societies generally implies a form of behaviourism: if we alter the social and physical structure we shall produce a new society which will be better and happier.

The nineteenth century also saw a conjunction between two important old-established ideas which made the utopian ideal more powerful: the new city as a garden. The New Jerusalem could thus be the paradise which had been the original Eden and which Christ promised even to the malefactor on the cross beside Him (St Luke 23.43). The garden had, in addition to this, strong associations with secular love both in Islamic and medieval literature, further strengthening its hold on the imagination as a desirable goal.

The architectural polemics of the first part of the twentieth century frequently emphasised the deterministic aspirations of their authors. Loos saw it in the abandonment of ornament: 'We have conquered ornament, we have won through to lack of ornamen-

26 Shaker tables and chair, Maine

44

tation. Look, the time is nigh, fulfilment awaits us. Soon the streets of the town will glisten like white walls. Like Zion, the holy city, the metropolis of heaven. Then we shall have fulfilment.' Le Corbusier characteristically put it at its most direct: ' . . . there does exist this thing called ARCHITECTURE, an admirable thing, the loveliest of all. A product of happy peoples and a thing which itself produces happy peoples.' Frank Lloyd Wright continually evoked a relationship between democracy and his architecture and the plans for Broadacre City: 'I am seeing and saying that organic architecture is the only true true architecture for democracy. Democracy will some day realize that life is itself architecture organic, or else both architecture and mankind will become in vain together.'

The second idea that is so evident is that evocation of the machine and its literal or implied relation to architecture. It again runs continuously through the writings of the pioneers of the modern movement in architecture and art. Probably the most rousing and

27 *Le Roman de la Rose*
miniature painting from a 15th
century copy.

widely publicised statement occurs in the Foundation Manifesto of the Futurists which appeared on the front page of *Le Figaro* on 20 February 1909: 'We declare that the splendour of the world has been enriched by a new beauty – the beauty of speed. A racing car with its bonnet draped with exhaust pipes like fire-breathing serpents – a roaring racing car, rattling along like a machine gun, is more beautiful than the winged victory of Samothrace.'

Van Doesberg writing in 1931 insisted that 'the machine is, *par excellence*, a phenomenon of spiritual discipline', and on another occasion: 'Since it is correct to say that culture in its widest sense means independence of Nature, then we must not wonder that the machine stands in the forefront of our cultural will-to-style . . . The new possibilities of the machine have created an aesthetic expressive of our time, that I once called "the Mechanical Aesthetic".' Le Corbusier's *Towards a New Architecture* makes continual references in both text and illustrations to engineering, to airplanes, to motor cars and liners. The analogies are not only visual:

'The airplane is the product of close selection.
The lesson of the airplane lies in the logic which governed the statement of the problem and its realization.
The problem of the house has not yet been stated.
Nevertheless there do exist standards for the dwelling house.
Machinery contains in itself the factor of economy, which makes for selection.
The house is a machine for living in.'

These lines, which stand as a rubric to a chapter on airplanes, sound like some extended syllogism and are clearly intended to demonstrate the absence of logical definitions in the statement of architectural problems; the lessons for architecture are to be found in engineering and in the clear, rational methods which are thought to be its basis. The imprint of these suggestions has been long lasting.

The visual references which Le Corbusier used embodied a further extension of the argument, namely that those objects which were designed to fit their purpose, and did so effectively, were also visually satisfactory; that the logic behind the design of the airplane not only made it fly but also made it beautiful. It could be said that Le Corbusier was following a line that Otto Wagner had more than ten years previously made clear: ' . . . every architect is going to have to come to grips with the postulate: "a thing that is unpractical cannot be beautiful." ' It is an assumption already expressed, for example, in the Shaker dictum: 'Anything may, with strict propriety, be called perfect which perfectly answers the purpose for which it was designed.' Machines, cars, airplanes, ships were seen as such perfect products, and the opposition between the success of their design method and the failure of the architectural design method was emphasised and often popularly accepted without anyone ever asking what exactly were the crucial elements of the method which produced motor cars or other admired engineering works such as bridges, dams or pylons, or indeed whether architects such as Le Corbusier when actually engaged on the design of a building pursued a method significantly different from that of their predecessors.

28 *Farman Airplane and Delage 1921 car as illustrated in 'Towards a New Architecture' by Le Corbusier*

It could be said that the architects I have chosen and the examples I have given are a selected sample and do not represent the whole story. The charge would be justified. It must on the other hand be remembered that these architects and their statements are those most often quoted, which have been transmitted as the representative story and which at the time they were made were seen as significant. A different tradition embodied in the work of Häring or Poelzig, for instance, has only much more recently been recognised as an important alternative strand of modern architecture. In a similar way the work of Lutyens in Great Britain or of Asplund in Sweden was thought to be outside the recognised canon and therefore barely relevant. It is only from the 1970s onwards that laudatory references to Lutyens, for example, were generally acceptable, special issues of magazines were devoted to his work and the most prestigious gallery showing modern art in London – the Hayward Gallery – mounted a special exhibition on his life and work. Twenty years previously Robert Furneaux Jordan, an architectural historian and then Principal of the Architectural Association School of Architecture, could refer to Lutyens as 'that dead-end kid of architecture' in a radio broadcast without arousing disagreement or even evoking comment.

29 *Hans Poelzig Chemical Factory, Luban, 1911–12*

30 Otto Bartning
Church, Constance, 1923

Similarly it was not until 1980 that there was a serious study of the work of Gunnar Asplund in English, soon followed by a number of other publications and then by an exhibition in London in 1988. What is probably more significant is that this exhibition and the various publications did not deal exclusively with Asplund's architectural designs which fell within the modern canon, such as his brilliant Stockholm Exhibition in 1930, but also with his more numerous buildings rooted in neo-classicism. It is these latter which are now, rightly or wrongly, seen as the most significant.

Because the process of design, whether in architecture or engineering, was uncertain, what mattered in the end to practitioners were the visual forms which might result from a belief in the importance of the machine; that there were signals which would make

31 Gunnar Asplund
Stockholm Exhibition, 1930

48

it obvious that this concern had been in the designer's mind; that there was a recognition of a style. Léger and others had shown that some components of machines could be used to make pictorial compositions. This was much more difficult in architecture. Even the most machine-like designs such as Clemente Busiri-Vici's Children's Seaside Colony (1932) or, later, Lloyd's in London by Richard Rogers (completed in 1986), which he called 'a machine inserted into the City', could not really be described as looking like contemporary machines or as having been produced by a sequence of design ideas which arose from a new method.

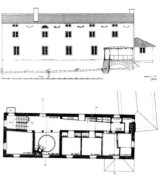

32 Gunnar Asplund
Villa Snellman, Djursholm,
1917–18

33 Clemente Busiri-Vici
Colonia Marina, XXVIII Ottobre,
Cattolica, 1932

6

The conclusions which I should like to be able to draw from the previous sections are that buildings considered in their entirety are not refutable, that architecture cannot therefore be a science, and that verbal prescriptions of buildings are unable to describe or specify their totality, or mathematical models to represent the sum of all existing relationships. I would also argue that the possibility that a meta-language might exist for architecture – that is to say, a language outside the one being used – is extremely doubtful except in the sense that one can be devised entirely after the event. It is obviously possible to imagine a language of three-dimensional coordinates and of codes embodying colour, texture and luminosity which could be used to define a space. But such a new non-verbal language could come into play only after the space had been designed or as a means of recording the way the space was being imagined during the process of design. The meta-language could not be used to specify the space without at the same time designing it. This seems to me an obvious logical problem which considerably undermines Christian Norberg-Schultz's avowed search for a meta-language, if I understand him rightly, in his influential book *Intentions in Architecture*.

The desire to devise verbal specifications stems from a number of points of view which are really not surprising. First of all, language is obviously the most common and generally the most readily understood medium of communication within any culture. To pass messages we usually talk or write, and such messages try to deal with the bulk of the world as we know it. To exempt architecture (or any other field of acitivity) is to make it into something special. Because we normally use words we should also like to be able to use them when dealing with buildings so that communication between architects and between architects and non-architects can happen in the most accessible medium. We naturally also communicate non-verbally – through dress, actions, the selection of symbols etc. – but verbal language is the only medium of communication in which we can conduct an argument and can conduct it in a way which will allow criticism to produce new results so that the process of argument (as distinct from the use of force, say) is itself a worthwhile activity. Any discussion of architecture must therefore resort to verbal language. This has clearly always been the case.

The need to rely on language is, I believe, especially crucial in the case of modern architecture since much of its intellectual underpinning came from the notion of functionalism, from the working assumption that there is a visible and definable match between use and form. Use requires description, frequently by non-architects; it is most readily achieved by the use of ordinary language. Only if this verbal basis is accepted can Louis Sullivan's much quoted dictum 'form follows function', which he derived from biology through the writings of Herbert Spencer, come into effect. Or what Christopher Alexander has more recently called (in a probably unconscious but direct verbal transliteration of Semper's 1853 formula): 'From a set of forces to a form'.

Sir John Summerson has gone so far as to argue in 'The Case for a Theory of Modern Architecture' that what distinguishes contemporary architecture from that of the past is that its 'source of unity . . . is in the social sphere, in other words in the architect's programme'. And the programme is a largely verbal statement. The sequence which leads up to this position may be surprising but is nevertheless historically traceable:

'From the antique (a world of form) to the programme (a local fragment of social pattern): this suggests a swing in the architect's psychological orientation almost too violent to be credible. Yet, in theory at least, it has come about; and how it has come about could very well be demonstrated historically. First the rationalist attack on the authority of the antique; then the displacement of the classical antique by the mediaeval; then the introduction into mediaevalist authority of purely social factors (Ruskin); then the evaluation of purely vernacular architectures because of their social realism (Morris); and finally the concentration of interest on the social factors themselves and the conception of the architect's programme as the source of unity – the source not precisely of forms but of adumbrations of forms of

51

undeniable validity. The programme as the source of unity is, so far as I can see, the one new principle involved in modern architecture. It seems to be the principle which can be discerned through the cloud of half-truths, aperçus and analogies which is the theoretical effluent – not a very nice word, I'm afraid – of the modern movement.'

Summerson is careful to point out that theory, which he labels 'a statement of related ideas resting on a philosophical conception of the nature of architecture', is 'an historical process with a life of its own in its own medium of words' and, most crucially, that he did not believe 'that forms somehow came out from the programme'; that 'where forms come from, as any art historian knows, is a very great mystery indeed'. If that is so, however, what exactly is implied by a sense of unity and a new principle?

Some time after making that statement at the Royal Institute of British Architects, Summerson took the opportunity, when speaking at the Architectural Association in London in 1960 after a talk by Reyner Banham, to refer to his RIBA lecture and to add:

'That talk was a considerable embarrassment to me, because when I had written about three-quarters of it, which consisted of a sort of shake-round of various historical ideas I had picked up from sundry books, I realised that there were seven different ways of ending the paper, one for every day of the week. As the paper was given on a Tuesday, I naturally chose the Tuesday version. It was philosophically entirely unsound, and so were all the others.'

The reasons for its unsoundness which were suggested were that 'such is the complexity of the human personality that I do not think we can begin to rationalise . . .' and also that 'there are such imponderable things as the pervading sense of novelty at any monment. People need design to change.' Neither, however, seriously cuts across Summerson's earlier arguments.

The wish to create in some way a close association between the verbally stated purpose and the eventual built form arises also, perhaps, from a desire to shift responsibility for the final outcome from the architect to the client. The wish may not be entirely conscious or ever acknowledged if stated in quite this way;

nevertheless I think it exists and should not be hidden. It is, for instance, implicit in the much publicised response of the establishment architect who said he was after all only like a tailor making different kinds of suits to order and that was all he could do. The more precise the formulation of needs, the more exhaustive the catalogue of user demands and the greater the suggestion of architectural fit, the easier it becomes to blame subsequent malfunctions on the initial brief. It is a logical outcome of the method.

That Summerson should have thought it opportune as a historian to summarise the position of the modern movement is only natural, but that he should have done so without questioning those particular premises is surprising. Especially as enough experience had been accumulated in the previous forty years or so to ask whether the assumptions corresponded with the current problems and whether, for that matter, they had ever done so. His disclaimer that theory and practice inhabited different worlds may be partially true but cannot really be taken to mean that they are entirely unrelated. The view that 'the most vital issues in the philosophy of art stem from the studio' seems to me more apposite.

If one looks at a number of building types, and especially those which might be described as being highly characteristic of the present, it soon becomes apparent that one of the key issues of any brief for such buildings is the very considerable difficulty in forecasting the patterns of use within the building during its expected life and in many instances even on completion of construction. This applies equally to buildings with highly complex requirements such as hospitals and to those with relatively simple functions such as air terminals, which are only a channelling system, and occasionally a holding area, for people and luggage between two different transport modes. A good deal of work on the planning of buildings for medical services has shown that in the modern hospital, where the planning and construction programme is extremely lengthy and changes in medicine are relatively rapid, what was decided at the outset may bear little relation to what is wanted when the hospital opens; ten years between the initial decision to build and the admission of the first patient is not at all unusual. Nor does the process of change stop when the construction of the building ceases. The need for indeterminacy in hospital design has been analysed at some length and various attempts have been made to achieve some measure of it in completed buildings. It seems that certain geometric arrangements allow for greater freedoms of increase in size and of change within the existing structure than others. These must not, however, sacrifice present convenience to some future but uncertain benefit, since the possibility that no growth and change will occur, or at least not for a very considerable period, must also be taken into account. This is particularly true in periods of economic stringency.

The hospital is one special case of a much more general situation; it has perhaps received rather more attention than other examples because of the very large investment of capital involved. What is true for hospitals is equally relevant to decisions on airport planning, the planning of new universities or the design of new schools.

The designers of the early stages of the programme which provided new buildings to deal with the creation of mixed-ability schools and the increased number of children in secondary education in Britain in the 1950s, for instance, were anxious to fragment

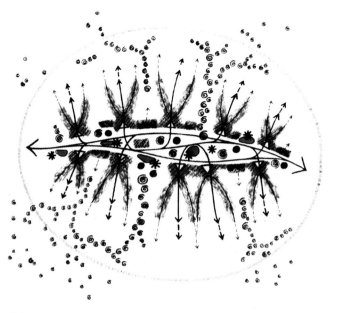

tthew, Johnson-
'artners
, University of Bath,

the large size of such comprehensive schools into recognisable social units. The house system, borrowed from the public schools where it corresponded to an actual functioning unit, led to the fragmentation of the building into pavilions, a literal translation of the social unit into houses. A comprehensive school of 2000 might have four or five house groups, each with its own name and each intent on making itself the focus of some kind of student loyalty. But when new educational attitudes emerged which, for example, wanted to alter the social system from houses containing children of all age groups to one where the year was the defined unit, or where there was to be a division into lower, middle and upper groups or even schools, where the social division as such was to play a very much less important role and the ease of access to some centrally placed library and resource centre was critical, then the precise tailoring of architectural form which had taken place originally became a hindrance. It was not that a division had been implied between different kinds of spaces (between social and teaching spaces in this instance) but that that distinction had been given a very specialised solution on the basis of a particular educational brief. Perhaps any other solution is difficult to imagine considering the attitudes of the time; nevertheless it is important to realise that the subsequent difficulties arise from a literal and accurate translation of particular elements of the verbal specification.

The existence of a well-prepared brief is thus in itself no guarantee of future success. In fact in many instances the essential statement of any brief would have to be that a precise definition of uses is impossible to formulate and undesirable to incorporate in any design specification; that the essence of the brief is that there is no brief. Nor did Summerson question whether, even when originally conceived, the notion of a close definition of a programme had high validity, quite apart from the more general problem as to whether there can ever exist a matching architectural answer to a set of criteria, however closely circumscribed these may be verbally or numerically.

If the brief is prepared by the client it is extremely likely that it is based on limited past experiences; if by the architect it is highly probable that it is the translation of what was first a visualisation back into verbal or numerical terms. In neither case does it seem to have the essential characteristics of that 'source of unity' which Summerson suggested. It must also be emphasised that if a brief is to be taken seriously, if it really is to have some social imperative, it must be precise and leave little room for ambiguity. Phrases such as 'the entrance space must allow enough room for movement at peak times' are meaningless as a brief, not just because they may state the obvious but equally because we have no agreed or defined measure for 'enough' or 'movement' for example.

Briefs have of course existed in the past. Palladio's clients, for instance, laid down certain demands and even made suggestions for the disposition of spaces. What they wanted from Palladio were proposals for facades, for proportional dimensions of rooms, for a whole set of visual decisions. These were in any case never strictly part of a brief, of the programme in Summerson's sense. What I take it Summerson is suggesting with his emphasis on 'the source of unity' is that the vast majority of the parts which make up a building will be the result of the stated programme and that it is this aspect which has introduced a new element into modern architecture.

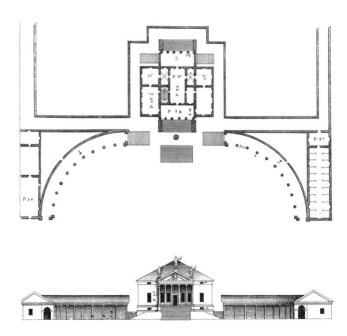

35 Andrea Palladio
Villa Badoer, 1556

It appears therefore that the guide to design which is currently provided by the client for the architect, and which has both a moral and an intellectual standing in the sense of being a justification for action, does not have the firm basis which orthodox architectural thinking demands of it. Once its position is weakened, or even seriously undermined, design decisions become more difficult and the burden of responsibility certainly more weighty.

7

If the orthodox assumptions on which the justification and the guidelines for design are based are found to be weak, and possibly even misleading, the question to be examined is whether there are other descriptions of the sequences in the design process and other guidelines to action which are more appropriate and which correspond more closely to the way in which design actually takes place. Two of the important criteria for such an alternative model are that it must not describe a process which starts from tightly circumscribed verbal or numerical definitions of the desired outcome, and that it must not presuppose a deterministic relationship between use and built form. Critical tests of such an alternative description should include that it bears an observable relationship to the way in which design is initiated and design decisions are taken, and that the application of such a model should avoid the most serious problems created by the use of the previous versions.

The suggestion I propose to make, and to pursue later, is that the initiation of a design is analogous to the way in which theories are put forward and amended; that in fact architecture – a built form – is in some way itself a theory in the sense of an explanation of a number of related phenomena rather than in the sense of the antithesis of practice. As in the case of theories in other fields, the explanatory power of a 'built theory' can vary depending on the degree of thoughtfulness with which it has been constructed, but perhaps also in relation to the phenomena which it tries to explain. Different levels of explanation may thus be appropriate to different situations. I believe that the differences in the intensity of explanation which we often sense may relate to the distinction which is sometimes made between building and architecture, and which, interestingly enough, forms the opening sentence of one of the best and most widely read histories of European architecture: 'A bicycle shed is a building; Lincoln Cathedral is a piece of architecture.'

In his paper 'A Realist View of Logic, Physics and History' Karl Popper puts forward a schema for the growth of theories which summarises the view he has elaborated over a number of years and to which he returns again and again. It takes the following form:

$$P_1 \rightarrow TT \rightarrow EE \rightarrow P_2$$

where ' "P" stands for "problem"; "TT" stands for "tentative theory"; and "EE" stands for "(attempted) error elimination", especially by way of critical discussion.' As the sequence shows, it does not necessarily solve problems but continually creates new problems, though clearly different ones, for P_2 must always differ from P_1. The existence and recognition of P_1 is crucial, however, not only because it is the beginning of the sequence but because the assumption that it is the effective starting point also provides a vital clue to the method and its philosophical background.

The recognition of the initial problem, of P_1, stems as a rule from an awareness that the phenomena being considered and the explanations being offered by the current theory no longer match in a way we find acceptable. The impetus to devise a new tentative theory, a new though probably partial solution of the problem, springs not from simply observing events but from looking at these from the standpoint of an already existing mental construct. We are not, in other words, neutral observers but theory-biased problem watchers. The distinction is vital.

It has its origin in Popper's rejection of Baconian inductive reasoning, namely that from repeated observations of events in the past we can infer future events and the regularities which govern the behaviour of these events. Hume had, in his discussion on causation, made a similar rejection of the process of reasoning from those instances which we know and which repeat themselves to other future ones which must of necessity be outside our experience. Yet Hume had at the same time to admit that we all believe that this will happen and that we continually function on the basis of such an erroneous expectation; that in fact we would probably not survive unless we did so. It was a paradox which led Hume to a position of scepticism, indeed of irrationality, in which he fell back on instinct as a foundation.

Popper clearly feels that his resolution of the paradox is one of his vital contributions to philosophy. He goes so far as to claim: 'I think that I have solved a major philosophical problem: the problem of induction . . . This solution has been extremely fruitful, and it has enabled me to solve a good number of other philosophical problems.' It is also from this solution, and the results which flow from it, that many of the applicatons outside philosophy can be derived.

The problem was first restated by Popper and a solution was then arrived at through the manner of the restatement:

'I formulated Hume's logical problem of induction as follows:

L_1 Can the claim that an explanatory universal theory is true be justified by "empirical reasons"; that is, by assuming the truth of certain test statements or observation statements (which, it may be said, are "based on experience")?

'My answer to the problem is the same as Hume's: No, we cannot; no number of true test statements would justify the claim that an explanatory universal theory is true.

'But there is a second logical problem, L_2, which is a generalization of L_1. It is obtained from L_1 merely by replacing the words "is true" by the words "is true or that it is false":

L_2 Can the claim that an explanatory universal theory is true or that it is false be justified by "empirical reasons"; that is, can the assumption of the truth of test statements justify either the claim that a universal theory is true or the claim that it is false?

'To this problem, my answer is positive: *Yes, the assumption of the truth of test statements sometimes allows us to justify the claim that an explanatory universal theory is false.*'

I have quoted this passage in full, partly to illustrate the simplicity of the argument, partly to allow this key point to be stated in Popper's own words and thus to emerge without ambiguity.

It is of course from the positive answer to L_2 that the statement on the line of demarcation can also be derived, although historically the two solutions were arrived at in reverse order: Popper formulated his ideas on demarcation in the winter of 1919–20 and those on induction not until 1927. Similarly many of the views on the political and social theories which are discussed in detail in *The Open Society and its Enemies* could be said to have their logical foundation in this solution of Hume's paradox. The fact that in most instances they derive from certain social democratic and humanitarian positions which go back to the Vienna of the 1920s does not invalidate the statement; it simply reinforces the proposition that in the sequence from P_1 to P_2 we always bring to P_1 some already existing outlook. There is no possibility of returning to the state of being Adam and Eve, nor would it prove very useful for we would lose the problem-solving experience of the intervening millennia.

Hume's problem arises because in our everyday existence we rely on expectations based on the belief that theories are true; we use them as guides to action. If we adopt Popper's position regarding the status of such theories, however, we must not be left in a sceptical and paralysed stance of inactivity; actions and decisions are still necessary even if some theories may be falsified in the future. Although it may be the duty of philosophy to question the ideas we hold and the assumptions we make about the world, it is not its task to destroy our capacity to act effectively within it. Indeed the opposite is the case. At any given time we may therefore be faced with a choice between competing theories, one of which, the existing theory, may be well entrenched.

The basis for such choices, Popper suggests, should be the degree to which any theory has successfully withstood testing, namely the extent to which it has survived serious attempts to falsify it. What is critical in the choices we make is thus the degree to which the function EE has previously been performed either by ourselves or others. Popper introduced the term 'corroboration' (which may sound more definite than he intended it to) 'for the degree to which a theory has been severely tested'. Moreover, because the testing of theories is an iterative process, raising new problems as we go along, 'the degree of corroboration of a theory has always a temporal index: it is the degree to which the theory appears well tested at the time t. This cannot be a measure of its verisimilitude, but it can be taken as an indication of how its verisimilitude *appears* at the time t, compared with another theory. Thus the degree of corroboration is a guide to the preference between two theories at a certain stage of the discussion with respect to their apparent approximation to the truth.' But having made the choice, we have not through such a decision said anything about the alleged truth of the selected theory.

Popper's work has itself been the subject of such criticism. Some of it stems from a profound disagreement with the historical evaluation which Popper gives of the ideas of Plato, Hegel and Marx, and the disagreement may go so far as to suggest that there has been a complete misunderstanding of the writings of those thinkers. It would be correct to add that such criticism comes largely from those who dogmatically hold the views which Popper attacks, and which he often attacks precisely because he believes that by their nature they are incapable of being criticised. There has also been a counter-attack by those committed to inductivist reasoning. The opposition is not unexpected but is irrelevant to this particular discussion, which tries to relate Popper's philosophical work to certain architectural problems. It would be unfortunate if the understandable opposition of Marxists to Popper's political views were to spill over to this attempt to discuss architectural issues. By making that distinction, I do not in any way wish to imply that architecture and politics are unrelated.

A more immediately relevant objection, and one foreseen by Popper, is that the new idea of corroboration – and especially the idea of choosing between competing theories on the basis of the degree of corroboration – simply, though perhaps furtively, reintroduces induction. Namely that we again make general statements from particular cases, except that these are now negative rather than positive judgements. But the differences are surely crucial: corroboration is seen as being tied to a particular time, a particular state of knowledge, and refutation proceeds by a sequence which raises none of the logical problems of inferring general laws from particulars. Somewhat analogous to this objection is the suggestion made by P. K. Feyerabend that 'the interpretation of an observation-language is determined by the theories which we use to explain what we observe, and it changes as soon as those theories change.' This presumably implies that all interpretations of observations are so 'theory-laden', and therefore so unstable, that they cannot even be used to falsify a theory. It is the kind of statement which brings any form of logical discussion of any theory, including that being put forward by Feyerabend, to a halt. The more important weakness of the statement is simply a historical and pragmatic one. The history of *science* has a very large number of instances in which theories once firmly held to be undeniably true have been shown to be erroneous, but hardly any cases of theories which, once seriously refuted, have later found a high level of corroboration. The graveyard of false theories is very extensive and resurrections are almost unknown.

One of the most sustained disagreements with Popper's view of science comes from Thomas S. Kuhn and was first put forward in *The Structure of Scientific Revolutions* in 1962; it was largely the subject of an International Colloquium in the Philosophy of Science in 1965. Kuhn sees science as primarily a puzzle-solving activity which at any one time is ruled by a paradigm. He takes paradigms to be 'universally recognized scientific achievements that for a time provide model problems and solutions to a community of practitioners'. He further believes that the switch from an old to a new paradigm 'cannot be made logically'. In this view historical periods are distinguished by their adoption of specific models, paradigms, which have connections to cultural and social manifestations and that these are from time to time disrupted by sudden revolutionary changes which are not solely due to the inconsistencies of the scientific theories. J. Habermas takes the position further and tries to analyse the social reasons which led to specific scientific points of view.

Neither criticism appears to me to invalidate Popper's position; both Kuhn's and to some extent Habermas's argument can be taken to describe one or several of the factors which make us realise the existence of a problem or make us choose a particular set of problems among a large number of varied problems. There is no doubt that our recognition of P_1 is theory-impregnated, and this is precisely Popper's point. I do not believe, however, that *all* the factors are those described by Kuhn and Habermas or that the traffic is only one way, that social forces affect science but that scientific thinking does not affect the social and cultural outlook. Science is part of our general culture and the interactions must of necessity be complex.

I also hold that Popper and Kuhn are not discussing quite the same thing, unless Kuhn were to argue that his view was as much a prescription as a description of the scientific method. Popper's argument focuses on the nature and character of science and any deductions about an appropriate method in the sciences follow from that view. Kuhn, on the other hand, emphasises the personal and institutional approaches which he believes exist among working scientists and he deduces from these what he believes to be the nature of 'normal science'. It is this correlation which allows Feyerabend to point out with amusement and sorrow that organised crime is also a puzzle-solving activity and that many of its aspects, both at the level of an organisation and of the individual safe breaker, could be described in a way identical to those which Kuhn uses to talk about 'normal science' and the 'individual scientist'.

Middle ground

8

The published writings of Karl Popper deal primarily with the philosophy of science, with the relation of philosophy to our political and social ideas, and with the theory of knowledge. None of the work so far released concerns itself specifically with art. There are frequent references to the importance of art and there is a brief discussion of music and of its development related to notions of creativity in Popper's autobiography. There is in fact an admission in the same book that he is musical but not visually minded, which may partly explain the omission. The most important attempt to make any kind of a bridge is due to Professor Gombrich (a personal friend ever since Popper's arrival in England) and appears in the 1956 Mellon Lectures, subsequently published as *Art and Illusion*. In these the psychology of perception and the problems of painting as representation were examined on the hypothesis that the artist cannot paint simply what he sees but that he invariably selects on the basis of an established schema. The beholder, moreover, has also to play a part in being predisposed to the same schema. Gombrich suggests that Popper's 'description of the way science works is eminently applicable to the story of visual discoveries in art'. He is able to illustrate his thesis from examples throughout the history of Western art and to demonstrate in particular to what extent well-known and established instances of depicting the world, say the human face or trees or buildings, affect subsequent representations even when these are drawn from life. Non-European painting would clearly provide an equally wide if not wider range of examples. The argument is not extended to sculpture, and architecture does not enter the discussion except in so far as it is a subject for painters.

Although Gombrich quotes with approval Constable's statement that 'painting is a science and should be pursued as an inquiry in the laws of nature', this does not mean that Popper's sequence from P_1 to P_2 is only relevant if we consider painting as a science. The line of demarcation between science and non-science based on the *necessity* for falsification can be separated from the notion that in science – and arguably in other pursuits – we proceed from seeing a

36 *Cathedral of Notre Dame, Chartes, engraving after a lithograph 1836 and modern photograph. The artist has elongated the facade in order to make it fit his view of Gothic.*

problem to a tentative solution, then go through a process of criticism which immediately or later reveals one or more new problems. The initial selection of a problem may be due to a number of causes but is most likely to arise from an absence of match between the explanation given by the current theory and all the facts currently available.

The applicability of the sequence outside science depends therefore on the extent to which it appears to be a reasonably accurate description and explanation of the process which actually takes place. Whether, if it were seriously applied in the architectural design process, it would also produce more generally acceptable results is an important but different problem.

The argument I wish to suggest is that the sequence is applicable outside science and is particularly relevant in the case of architecture. I believe, however, that this requires an extension of the definition of 'facts' to include 'expectations'; that we need to widen the statement describing the principal causes which lead to the realisation that there is a problem. Our dissatisfaction with the currently available explanation – whether that explanation is a theory or some other explanatory statement of a situation – is due either to a possible mismatch between the facts which are now available or to our changing expectations of the answers which that explanation should provide, or to both. New facts and new expectations may arise or be perceived which cause an absence of fit between these and the available explanation. We are then prodded, or even driven, to find alternative solutions.

The important point is that the sequence from P_1 to P_2 remains intact and that it is only the initial promptings which are different. That these should

37 Le Corbusier
Notre-Dame du Haut, Ronchamp
perspective from south-east, March
1951

not be the same as in science seems to me hardly surprising and is surely simply a reflection of the difference in the nature of the answers we expect from physics, for instance, and architecture. One of the highly significant differences is that in science we believe the new theory to have a greater explanatory power than the one it supplants – which may be the reason for choosing and accepting it. This is not necessarily the case in art or architecture; there we accept the new answer, when we accept it, not because of its greater power but because of its greater relevance; it seems a more apposite solution.

38 Acropolis, Athens view from the west

Why we do so is a complex problem; the fact that we do so seems to be amply testified by the continuous but marked changes which have occurred throughout history and by the attitude we adopt to these differences. We do not assume that Le Corbusier's chapel at Ronchamp can be preferred to the Parthenon on the Acropolis, to take two religious buildings on a hillside plateau as an example. Irrespective of their possible ranking on some architectural value scale, assuming for the moment that such a scale exists, we simply accept their differences because of the gap in time between them. To take a reverse example, we are somewhat uncertain about the appropriateness of the precisely repeated Doric temple which constitutes Leo von Klenze's design of the Walhalla, that curious memorial to the great men of German history on a hill above the Danube at Regensburg which was inaugurated in 1842. Semper had previously already expressed doubt about such a copy. Our most common reaction in architecture is the opposite to that in science: we often prefer the old to the new.

Two important consequences follow from these assumptions. The first is that the history of architecture in no way represents some linear progress as might, arguably, the history of medicine. Where attempts have been made to show the opposite, it has been necessary to restrict the meaning of architecture so that it is synonymous with structure, for example, and its capacity to span a space. It then becomes just possible to establish a more or less linear sequence of increasing ability to design, calculate and build structures able to cover without intermediate supports larger and larger spaces. There is no doubt that the dome of St Peter's encloses a very much greater

39 Leo von Klenze Walhalla, Regensburg, 1816–42

40 Leo von Klenze
Walhalla, Regensburg, 1816–42

area than the roof of the Parthenon or that the steel frames of the Galerie des Machines at the Paris Exposition of 1889 in turn greatly surpassed St Peter's. However, we do not normally equate such an ability to provide cover with architecture or evaluate architecture on a scale related to the span of its roof or floors.

The second, and probably more important, consequence is that the sequence from P_1 to P_2 avoids many of the problems of language and definition because both P_1 and P_2 and the intermediate tentative solutions can remain in their original 'language'. We do not always have to be involved with problems of translation and correspondence rules. This, as has already been pointed out, is particularly crucial in the case of architecture where verbal descriptions are especially difficult both as prescriptions of requirements and as part of the design-thinking process. We are able to recognise the existence of an architectural problem, however stimulated, and having through criticism of the present solution diagnosed some of the errors, we are then able to provide a new tentative architectural answer. Both the problem and the solution are architectural and can therefore be compared with each other.

41 Cottanci and Dutert
Palais des Machines (Galerie des Machines) International Exhibition, Paris, 1889

What it is that we see as errors at any one time may vary widely, nor is there always likely to be unanimity as to what the main errors are. The mismatch between the current answer and our expectations may come from social and economic needs, from technical performance, from visual and

70

stylistic demands or a combination of these. What is perhaps recent is a standpoint which suggests that a change in one aspect demands corresponding changes in all other aspects. It is an important claim of contemporary architecture that the social, technical and visual elements of any solution are inextricably entwined. That the proclaimed views and the executed buildings lack such a correspondence has by now been well established.

Part of the desire to enmesh all these aspects stems again, I suggest, from the utopian tradition which has exercised such a strong influence on architectural attitudes and in many ways continues to do so even when any specific utopian vision is no longer present. Part of its power comes from precisely this all-embracing attitude which derives from the ideals on which any utopia is based. Thomas A. Reiner has aptly summarised this as:

'Utopian thinking embraces a number of critical themes. First, the utopian mode is one which looks at the *totality of man's experience*, or at least a large segment of life. Second, it is a *clear* vision of the future which implies rather *basic changes* in fundamental relations, institutions and processes. Third, the utopian style is one which transcends simple adaptation to exogenous forces, it is a response to *explicitly formulated* values, objectives, and criteria, as these themselves may be in flux.'

I have italicised the phrases which I believe give the utopian vision its strength but which are also its potential dangers. Both aspects of this position have deeply affected architectural thought since the 1920s. The attitude implied in the quotation from Professor Reiner's essay is of course the opposite to that suggested by the P_1 to P_2 sequence; it assumes that we are able to see a clearly defined ideal goal towards which we can design, rather than continually correcting our current problems and accepting that the answers we are likely to provide will raise new problems in the future; that it is in their very nature that this should happen. The difference between these two positions is fundamental and critical to architectural design.

9

The design process and its immediate outcome can be roughly equated with the tentative solution, the tentative theory step, in the move from P_1 to P_2. It represents the elaboration of a new and alternative hypothesis, irrespective of the degree to which it differs from the previous answer.

Any discussion of the design process in these terms also presupposes that it is a problem-solving process in which decisions are possible and that these are not entirely predetermined by the definition of the problem; that there is no inevitable outcome. Whether these problems are self-imposed or the result of external demands is at the moment immaterial. J. F. Blondel's unease that there were such considerable differences in the designs for the completion of the Louvre may raise a sympathetic response even today, but his argument that 'if every architect had designed his submission rationally, there would only have been very slight disparities between them' is nevertheless untenable. Design presupposes that there are always alternatives which are available and that a deliberate selection is possible and indeed necessary. It is assumed to be necessary because different choices lead to different solutions and these cannot all be seen as having equal value. Unless it is to be the result of pure chance, the notion of selection must be based on preferences and these in turn suggest the need to depend on conscious value judgements or on the existence of well-entrenched and unquestioned values or, probably most frequently, on some combination of these two positions. It is worth emphasising again that however these selections are made the eventual outcome of the design – a building, a garden, a chair – cannot be rated as the best solution, either in an absolute sense or in the sense of a set of unique conditions, but only as the most preferred in those circumstances. It is assumed to match our critical expectations most closely; no higher claims can be made.

The values which we hold and which inevitably influence the decisions we make come not only from those domains with which we traditionally associate the idea of values, the social and moral spheres, but also from technology and from visual predilections,

from the existence of a style. The current state of
technology obviously puts limitations on what is
possible or expedient and may totally exclude certain
solutions even if these can be imagined. But within
the range of the possible or even difficult we still
make technological choices on the basis of value
judgements that lie outside the realm of strict
technical appropriateness. When Le Corbusier, for
instance, used concrete in his buildings of the
immediate post-war period – the Unité d'Habitation
at Marseilles and the chapel at Ronchamp – the
formwork was made of rough wooden planks. The
patterns which such sawn shuttering gave the
concrete surface differed considerably from that
achieved by plywood and this became the principal
characteristic feature of 'béton brut'. What started as
a recourse to basic available materials in a period of
post-war shortages and economic stringency became
a visual hallmark of up-to-dateness. Architects began
using boarded formwork even when plywood or steel

43 Le Corbusier
Unité d'Habitation, Marseilles,
1945–52
roof

sheet was readily available and as a rule less expensive than the more primitive method requiring a great deal of labour. Values placed on appearance determined a technical choice and, one suspects, did so initially in Le Corbusier's case.

The process also works in an inverse way. There is no doubt that for many climates the sash window is an eminently sensible way of providing an opening; it allows highly controlled ventilation at top and bottom even when it is raining, it is constructionally simple because it has a balanced vertical sliding action which does not put any large and eccentric stresses on the frame, it is reasonably easy to clean on both sides, it does not protrude beyond the face of the building, nor does it interfere with curtains or blinds on the inside of the room. Yet because it had strong and immediate stylistic associations with Georgian architecture its use in buildings which were intent on declaring their twentieth century characteristics during the 1920s and 1930s was virtually ruled out. Visual values excluded certain technical choices.

We are of course continually involved in making just such design choices and this is not in any way a recent phenomenon. Semper, for example, who at one level strove for what he assumed to be rationality in design was at the same time able to voice a not uncommon nineteenth-century point of view, that iron was not a noble material and therefore not fit to be used in monumental architectural works. Henri Labrouste's use of cast and wrought iron for the columns and roof of the Bibliothèque Ste Geneviève in Paris of 1843–1851 caused disapproval not so much because the material was unfamiliar or in any way structurally inappropriate but because it was employed in such an important building as a library. The same was true for a mid-nineteenth century proposal for the design of an iron church. Nor have we entirely lost that feeling; apart from such examples as Otto Bartning's church in Cologne of 1928 and Mies van de Rohe's chapel at the Institute of Technology in Chicago there is hardly an important religious building of the recent past in which steel construction plays an important visual role. A considerable programme of church building took place in such a technologically advanced country as West Germany during the 1950s and 1960s yet there is hardly a significant example in steel; most of the work is in

44 *William Slater*
Design for an Iron Church, 1856
'*The iron structures so familiar to our eyes in railway sheds are altogether unecclesiastical in character and associations, and, like the Crystal Palace, fall within the province of engineering rather than of architecture. But undoubtedly they show a legitimate use of that material, and develop, according to sound principles, its special properties and characteristics. The present design is an attempt to show how a churchlike building may be constructed in iron, without, on the one hand, abandoning architectural forms, or, on the other, violating the essential laws which ought to regulate the employment of this, or indeed of any, material.*'
The Ecclesiologist, XX, 1856

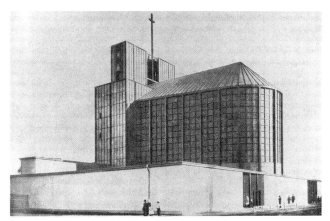

45 Otto Bartning
Church at Cologne Exhibition, 1928

reinforced concrete. We find it difficult, it would seem, to make an easy association between the idea of church and the expression of steel structure. Mies's aphorism: 'We refuse to recognise problems of form, but only problems of building' ignores the fact that the problem of building is also one of making choices, including choices of material which in Mies's own terms affect form. It might therefore be more accurate to suggest that there is no problem of building which is not also a problem of form.

46 Mies van der Rohe
St Saviour Chapel, Illinois Institute of Technology, Chicago, Illinois 1949–52

75

The late seventeenth and eighteenth century term 'taste', which has now perhaps acquired a certain uncomfortable association with effete sensibility, included in its original meaning precisely this function of judgement and discernment, the balancing of decisions in terms of their eventual outcome, which we continually perform whatever label we care to give the activity. Corresponding decisions but with different outcomes are made by the beholder; both the maker and the receiver are involved in what Clement Greenberg has called, in his Bennington seminars, the aesthetic experience. And the crucial element of this

'aesthetic experience *is* judging, is making judgements of taste, is liking or not liking, getting or not getting satisfaction in different degrees; an aesthetic intuition doesn't just coincide with, isn't just consubstantial with, a verdict of taste: it means a verdict of taste. . . And because they consist in judging, these decisions are of a special kind in their very character as decisions. Just as an aesthetic judgement can't be separated from its object, so an aesthetic decision can't be separated from its result: one is the other, without any gap between them. When the artist makes an aesthetic decision he experiences its results in the decision itself, and at the same time. And it makes no difference whether that decision stays locked in his mind or whether it gets precipitated in an object, an act, or a symbolized meaning.'

Greenberg goes on to add, in an aside which reveals something of his understanding of the workings of the studio:

'In the context of my argument it makes no difference. But this isn't to say that many of the most fruitful decisions do not come as a feedback in the course of making an actual object or arriving at an act or symbolized meaning. The artist receives judgement-decisions – inspiration, if you like – from his medium as he works on it; one judgement-decision, as the artist himself sees, hears, or reads it, gives rise to another and reacts on a previous one or cancels it out or cancels itself out.'

The particular set of values which guides our design choices, which informs our judgement, constitutes a style. It is this set of visual precepts which makes us select some forms in preference to others. This applies to those creating and to those receiving the work. And the influence which these values exert is strong and pervasive. As Wolfflin correctly saw it, 'even the most original talent cannot proceed beyond certain limits which are fixed for it by the date of its birth'.

The interesting point, however, is not that this should be the case – it is a statement which could be said to be self-evident – but why it should be so. The reason, I suggest, is that the artist like the scientist is primarily involved in deductive thinking; that art also needs some hypothesis as a starting point, some guideline which makes it possible to select from the endless array of observations and materials. Or as Gombrich suggested in terms of his own argument:

47 *Rock cut interior, Hypogeum of Hal Saflieni, Malta, 5000 BC.*
The rock interior follows the wall and frame construction of above ground buildings

'Our formula of schema and correction, in fact, illustrates the very procedure. You must have a starting point, a standard of comparison, in order to begin that process of making and matching and remaking which finally becomes embodied in the finished image. The artist cannot start from scratch but he can criticize his forerunners.'

And not only his forerunners but also himself and his earlier work.

The most frequently used and the most readily available point of departure is, therefore, the work of the present and the past, including, and often primarily, one's own work. There is not only the style of a period but equally discernible personal styles within that general framework: personal value systems which inform the choices of individuals. Occasionally the starting point is some related work or natural object which is seen at that moment as having some equivalence in terms of the problem to be solved and which fits within the hypothesis being elaborated. For instance, the shapes and details seen on ships are transferred to buildings and become the characteristic element of a period, or Paxton's

48 *K F Schinkel*
Kaufhaus project, Berlin, 1827, designed after Schinkel's travels to England in the summer of 1826

49 Kings Stanley Mill, Stroud Valley, 1761

recognition of the structural appropriateness of the leaf of the giant water lily *Victoria Regia* at Chatsworth becomes the clue to creating a roofing system.

It is the work of the past and especially of the immediate past which as a rule provides the most accessible and most easily assimilated point from which to start. As the familiarity of new work shows, the extent of the move away from that starting point is usually very small. What is recognised as innovation is in fact a more marked shift from that base line and is very often due to a new point of departure not in common currency. The brilliant and admired insight lies frequently not so much in the making of a new answer as in the discovery of a different platform from which to mount an attack on an old problem.

10

Among the great architectural figures of the first two-thirds of this century, Le Corbusier is often assumed to have shown the most original talent in the sense of having produced architectural forms more novel than those of his contemporaries. Whether the supposition is correct is another matter; the important point is that it is made. It is perhaps abetted by the fact that Mies van de Rohe acknowledged his debt to Karl Friedrich Schinkel in particular and the neo-classical period in general, and that in the work of Frank Lloyd Wright the influence of Japanese and Central American architecture is often evident even though totally absorbed within Wright's personal idiom. Yet on any evidence Le Corbusier was an architect deeply rooted in the French classical tradition and strongly imbued with the forms of Mediterranean buildings.

In 1911 at the age of 24 Le Corbusier spent 21 days on Mount Athos, the peninsula north of Salonika on which the Orthodox Church has built a group of monasteries during the last thousand years. Within

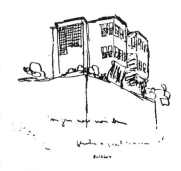

50 Le Corbusier
*Turkish wooden house, sketch,
Bosphorus, 1911*

51 Monastery of Stavronikita,
Mount Athos, 16th century

52 *Le Corbusier*
View of Simonopetra, Mount Athos,
1911

them a Byzantine way of life has survived both at the level of daily ritual and as a building tradition. No visitor can escape the deeply ingrained attitudes of the all-male religious community which lives in the monasteries and hermitages, nor avoid the visual impact of buildings set between sea and mountains. Le Corbusier sketched what he saw and his published notebooks record his continuous interest in such Mediterranean forms throughout his travels. The similarity between the forms of the Athonite monasteries and those of La Tourette, the Dominican monastery which he designed in 1957 on a sloping hillside near Lyon, is clear and perhaps hardly surprising. Both have courtyard plans, both place the monks' cells as a repetitive element at the upper level which overhangs the base of the building, both emphasise the agglomerated nature of the building complex. It can of course be argued that such parallels are natural since in both instances we are dealing with buildings serving very similar functions even if we ignore the different religious groups involved. Yet La Tourette is much closer in appearance and general character to a monastery on Athos than to a nineteenth-century monastery that might have been built in France or to the Baroque monasteries of the Upper Danube, for example, which are not only closer in time and locality but are widely known and more readily available as sources than the remote buildings of a little-visited Greek peninsula.

Le Corbusier in other words side-stepped using the obvious model, a building familiar to his clients and himself in the sense that they might have shown it to him and pointed out its merits and faults, and used as his point of departure a model known to him from the past but certainly not in common currency. Much of its novelty, of its originality and impact, stems therefore from this lateral shift in finding a new and different, and in some ways unexpected, clue to starting the design. The components of the design go back to Le Corbusier's own previous work, to architectural forms with which he was familiar and which perhaps he felt confident in handling. The precast concrete cladding and balcony rails of the monks' rooms are very close to those of the Unité d'Habitation at Marseilles, parts of the building are clear of the ground as in a great many other designs

53 *Le Corbusier*
Sainte-Marie de la Tourette, near
Eveux-sur l'Arbrêsle, 1953–59

by Le Corbusier, and the colours of the chapel follow the vocabulary of strong primary colours which he had used for a considerable number of years.

Despite the architect's strong personal involvement with the Abbé and his community which has been fully recorded and his study of their needs over a period of several years, what stands above the meadows at Eveux-sur-l'Arbrêsle is in its architectural form derived from assumptions about suitable building forms which preceded the posing of the problem. Hypotheses were to some extent already formulated, were in existence restricting the area of choice, and were then used to produce this particular result. This seems to me to be highly analogous to the processes of deductive thinking.

It might be objected that any parallel between Simonopetra or Chilandar and La Tourette is not very informative since the building programme deals with a static, perhaps even archaic, function in which tradition is highly valued and in which recourse to earlier and arguably more primitive forms would be approved and indeed encouraged. Le Corbusier's model shift would on this argument not be rated as original but as expected. The real test would be some more recent and much less well established building programme in which the need to innovate was seen to be immediately necessary, in which in a sense it could not be escaped.

Of all of Le Corbusier's executed works, the Unité d'Habitation of 1947–52 could be said to have involved the newest kind of design brief and one far removed from the influence of an individual patron as might be the case in a private house. The idea of a large apartment block which would also contain a number of communal functions – in the case of Marseilles, shops, nursery school, hotel – had been developed in the Soviet Union in the immediate post-revolutionary period, but there were few built examples which could act as adequate precedent. Le Corbusier would have been familiar with these from his visit to Moscow in 1928. The earlier Russian designs were an attempt to solve the enormous housing shortage in Moscow after 1917 and a way of socially and politically influencing the residents through the existence of communal libraries, classes and other activities. The communal spaces were also in some way to compensate for the very small area

54 Le Corbusier
L'Unité d'Habitation, Marseilles,
1947–52

55 Moses Ginzburg
*Group of living units and integral
collective services, research project,
1928*

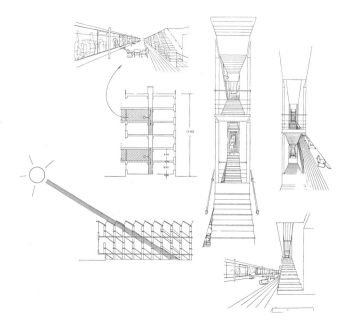

which could be provided for each flat. The Unité
d'Habitation more than thirty years later was also an
attempt to deal with the post-war demand for
housing and to provide for the social activities which
were lacking in existing French apartment buildings
and in the newer suburbs. The notion was to create a
small vertical town, a community within a building
set in an open landscape.

Although the social idea was relatively new and
untried, neither the idea of such a functional
organisation nor the suggested architectural structur-
ing were entirely novel. Both could be found in the
royal palaces and, as far as Le Corbusier was
concerned, particularly in the great châteaux of
France. As John Winter once remarked to me on
returning from the Loire: 'If you look at Chambord,
all of Marseilles is there' – a building as a contained
free-standing entity within which many disparate
activities happen, set within a landscape free from
other buildings and in scale with the broad expanses
of uncultivated nature; a building articulated into
base, middle and top with an exuberant emphasis on
its roof; a building of both violent sculptural forms
and repetitive elements.

The social organisation suggested by Marseilles
and Chambord and the architectural forms common

*56 Chateau de Chambord, Loire,
early 16th century*

82

to both can also be found in the ocean liner. The Unité can indeed be read as a great ocean liner anchored in the fields. There is considerable evidence of Le Corbusier's enormous interest in boats, particularly ocean liners, in the text and illustrations of *Towards a New Architecture*. I am not aware of any direct evidence that Chambord or any other châteaux or the forms of any ship were in Le Corbusier's mind when he designed Marseilles, the first built solution to the problem of mass housing which he had considered over a number of years. The only inference I wish to suggest is that the particular solution to this general problem came, like La Tourette, through a model which although familiar to Le Corbusier was to others unexpected and that the acclaimed originality came again from such a model shift. The basis of the design process seems, therefore, to be no different whether the problem is, as in the case of a monastery, within a long-standing tradition or, as in the case of large-scale public housing, of relatively recent origin.

57 The Liner 'France' as illustrated in 'Towards a New Architecture' by Le Corbusier

11

There are fortunately instances where direct evidence of origins is available and where it has been carefully documented.

Sinan, the greatest architect of the Ottomans and a close contemporary of Leonardo and Michelangelo, wrote in the autobiography he dictated:

'Architects in Christian countries may rank themselves above Mohammedans in technical skill, owing to the failure of the latter to achieve anything approaching the dome of St Sophia. This assertion of insurmountable difficulty has wounded the author of these writings. However, with God's help and the Sultan's mercy, I have succeeded in building a dome for Sultan Selim's mosque which is four ells greater in diameter and six ells higher than that of St Sophia.'

Hagia Sophia thus acted as both challenge and model, although designed by Anthemis of Tralles and Isidorus of Miletus just over a thousand years earlier for a different religion. It was part of the known stock and clearly worthy of emulation;

58 Sinan
Sultan Selim Mosque, Edirne, 1569–
1575

59 *Anthemis of Tralles and Isidorus of Miletus Hagia Sophia, Constantinople, 532–537*

Mehmet the Conqueror had after all specifically ordered its preservation when he entered Constantinople in 1453.

A number of similar recorded instances are available from other visual arts where it seems that models play an equally important role.

Francis Bacon has described in his conversations with David Sylvester how the photographs by Muybridge showing the sequences of human and animal movement have closely influenced his paintings in both subject matter and execution. Francis Bacon is widely considered as amongst the most original British painters of his period. Originality and innovation are thus not in any way related to the rejection of existing models, nor can they be based on the belief that by a process of inductive reasoning a mind cleared of all existing solutions will produce startlingly new and appropriate answers. On the contrary, the opposite appears to be the case.

60 *Eadweard Muybridge Sequence of photographs from 'The Human Figure in Motion', 1887*

61 *Francis Bacon Crucifixion, triptych, 1965*

62 African Tribal Mask given to Maurice Vlaminck in 1905

A friend of the painter Modigliani, describing his mental state around the year 1911, wrote:

'At this time Modigliani was crazy about Egypt. He took me to the Louvre to look at the Egyptian section; he assured me that everything else, "tout le reste", didn't deserve any attention. He drew my head in the attire of Egyptian queens and dancers, and he seemed completely carried away by the great Egyptian art. Obviously Egypt was his last passion. Very soon after that he became so original that looking at his canvases you didn't care to remember anything. This period of Modigliani's is now called *La période nègre*.'

The examples of Francis Bacon and Amedeo Modigliani were chosen not only because there is in both instances clear evidence for the particular process under discussion but mainly because there is no doubt in either case about their reputation for originality. Superficial reasoning might easily suggest that the reliance on models, on the acceptance of some hypothesis, would only occur in the case of well-established routine solutions in which the move from the previous answer was barely discernible and that what distinguished innovatory action more than anything else was giving up this process and starting afresh. Neither personal histories nor the histories of various periods indicate, however, that this is so.

The influence of African art on Picasso and Braque or of Islamic arabesque and calligraphy on Matisse are well known and need not be elaborated in a discussion of architecture. The African tribal mask which was given to Maurice Vlaminck in 1905 and which was bought by André Derain and shown to both Picasso and Matisse with such effect can still be identified. In very much the same way the effect of the growing awareness of Japanese art, and particularly of the Japanese print, on the French painters of the late nineteenth century, and later on the arts in general through the Art Nouveau movement, is by now familiar and does not require a great deal of imaginative effort to retrace or understand. We have since become so familiar with the sources that the novelty of the model shift no longer holds the same surprises. But it does require an imaginative attitude to become fully aware of the startling unfamiliarity which a Hokusai woodcut would have had in the

86

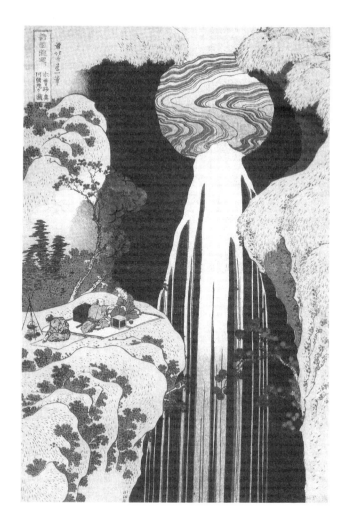

Paris of the 1870s. What is critical to the argument is that in each of these instances the seemingly revolutionary changes in direction were dependent on the ability to have recourse to some existing visual model which was unfamiliar and fresh in the sense that it allowed a new line of exploration, that it provided the beginning of a new hypothesis on how we look and describe the world. Why there should be a need for such changes and how these come about is another and perhaps more difficult question, to be looked at shortly. It is certainly a crucial point which cannot be escaped if the argument is to be useful to an understanding of how the design process is performed and why it does not always produce similar results as Blondel had wanted.

64 *Boston and Lowell Railroad 'Car House', Lowell, Mass. 1835*

Undoubtedly the most extended and probably the most stimulating and far-reaching change to an alternative but pre-existing model which has occurred in European history is the Renaissance. The ability to go back to a source which had also the stamp of being in some way original and pure proved extremely fruitful, perhaps especially because initially that source was imprecise and certainly sparse. The number of new interpretations, of novel reinterpretations and therefore of adaptations proved to be very large and could be modified regionally to suit the considerable array of uses so that a limited number of elements could be employed as much in architecture as in furniture. The vagueness of the evidence available from the antique at the beginning of the Renaissance was, I would suggest, essential to its usefulness as a model. Had Roman and particularly Greek structures been complete, familiar and currently used buildings, their capacity to serve as a springboard would have been greatly diminished, perhaps even totally negated. What has recently been important to Francis Bacon or Picasso was that the Muybridge photographs or the carvings of West Africa were able to provide clues to new ways of perceiving and making objects without having already created all the answers. In very much the same way the literary sources of Vitruvius discussing architecture and the only partially visible remains of classical antiquity provided hints and gave the outline of a model without having pre-empted the need to continue to solve problems. Radical model shifts are generally in the direction of hypotheses

(a)

65 *James Stuart and Nicholas Revett 'The Antiquities of Athens'*
Vol II, a new edition, London, 1825
(Vol I first published in 1762, Vol II after 1788)
(a) Plate XXVII, west front, 'Temple of Minerva Polias, (Erechtheion)
(b) Plate XI, mouldings, Parthenon

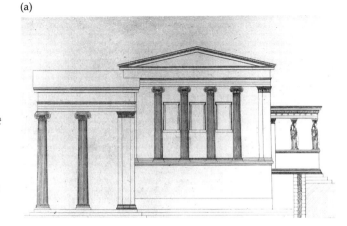

which by their nature are as yet unexplored for the purpose for which they have been chosen. Perhaps only if they have that quality are they seen as worthwhile sources.

Ruskin's vehement outburst in *The Stones of Venice* that Renaissance architecture was 'an architecture

(b)

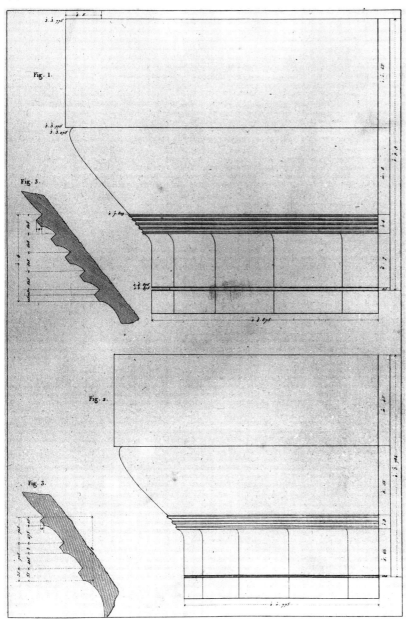

66 *K F Schinkel*
Project for a Palace at Orianda,
Crimea, 1838
view of the terrace by the sea.
Glass in bronze frames between the
columns on the right provides
protection from the weather

invented, as it seems, to make plagiarists of its architects, slaves of its workmen, and sybarites of its inhabitants; an architecture in which intellect is idle, invention impossible. . . ' was both wrong and misguided, quite apart from being illogical since he was simultaneously advocating Venetian and Florentine Gothic as apposite models. It was exactly because plagiarism was by the nature of the available evidence impossible in the fifteenth and sixteenth centuries that the antique could exert such a powerful influence.

When in the middle years of the eighteenth century Roman and Greek remains began to be excavated and to some extent restored, and more accurate recon-

90

67 *Thomas Jefferson*
University of Virginia,
Charlottesville, Virginia, 1817–26

structions became possible as a result of archaeological activity, it could be argued that a new but more precise model had become available which resulted in neo-classicism. Yet I believe that it can be maintained that even the more accurate descriptions which Stuart and Revett were able to provide in 1762 in their *Antiquities of Athens* or Robert Adam of Diocletian's palace at Spalato were still in no way the solution to the problems which faced neo-classical architects. Similarly the known examples of Roman temples or triumphal arches were in no way clear and immediately usable solutions to the problems which Alberti faced in the middle of the fifteenth century designing the façades of Christian churches. The number of times it was possible or even thought desirable to use a Doric temple in its entirety, as in von Klenze's Walhalla, was strictly limited. Even in that instance what was built in the nineteenth century was something that did not exist, namely a Doric temple roofed and complete. Schinkel's Altes Museum in Berlin or his design for a palace on the Black Sea coast or Jefferson's design for the University of Virginia were all far removed from any possible classical precedent and were so of necessity. It was probably exactly this absence of a close match between the results produced by the inspirational source and the solutions required in the late eighteenth and early nineteenth century which made neo-classicism so fruitful both in Europe and elsewhere.

Perhaps periods characterised by eclecticism such as the latter part of the nineteenth century during which Gottfried Semper practised, but which he found so objectionable, are those in which there are numerous and relatively rapid explorations for an alternative but acceptable and useful model. It may therefore be a process which is not to be castigated but which occurs at frequent intervals in architectural

68 Augustus Welby Pugin
St Barnabas Cathedral, Nottingham,
1841–44

69 Raymond Erith
King's Walden, Bury, Hertfordshire,
1969–71

history and is at certain times merely more diversi-fied. Paradoxically the real objection to some forms of eclecticism, to some aspects of the Gothic revival for instance, may have been not so much that we no longer lived in a medieval world wearing doublet and hose but that the answers which Victorian Gothic-revival architects were able to provide were too close to what was already in existence and in daily use in the local church. What may cause the casual twentieth-century observer to think of a revivalist church such as Pugin's Cathedral Church of St Barnabas in Nottingham of 1841–44 as a fake is not so much that is is based on the earlier model but that that particular model, although no longer current, is yet far too familiar and already accepted.

In a very similar way, any unease occasioned 150 years later by the work of Raymond Erith and his followers may not be due so much to disapproval of the results as visual compositions but to a sense of the staleness of the expression which so closely mimics a well-known model, a model which we clearly associate with the past and which we instantly know to be related to a particular historical period.

It is therefore vital to recognise the difference between mimicry and the use of one or several models within the design process. If that difference were not always present, there would be no need to move beyond P_1 in the Popperian sequence. In fact there would be no P_1 as a problem; we would simply repeat what is there. But this is not the way we design, however much we admire the architecture of previous periods, nor is it the way historical sequences have actually evolved.

12

The fact that such changes occur at recognisable intervals can hardly be in dispute: the most elementary textbook of architectural history will enumerate and describe the styles which characterise different periods. The chances are that the more elementary its treatment, the more likely it is to treat each model as an established norm and to neglect the periods of transition; in other words to see abrupt changes rather than tentative beginnings which sometimes take hold and become accepted over a wide range of buildings, though not necessarily all. The beginnings of Renaissance architecture, for example, are usually described in such terms, but it should be remembered that Italian architects of the fifteenth century were familiar with the Tuscan Proto-Renaissance of the twelfth century, as at San Miniato al Monte in Florence, or with Romanesque buildings – themselves derived from Roman sources – in Ravenna, Venice and elsewhere.

70 *San Miniato al Monte, Florence, 11th century*

71 *Santa Maria de Naranco, Monte Naranco, Oviedo, Asturias, 842–50*

To acknowledge the existence of a model shift does not explain its origin, however, nor the fact that such shifts appear to occur in most societies, though at different frequencies and with different amplitudes. Although it may not be possible to define all the causes which produce such changes, it may be useful to look into this particular problem further, in order to at least understand the process. An exhaustive list of reasons may in any case not be necessary to gain an insight, nor can such a list perhaps ever be defined with any degree of certainty. But this is a difficulty which architecture shares with all historical problems: we can never be certain of all the reasons which led up to known events. What will be most helpful to our understanding of the sequences which have occurred in the past, and which are also likely to be happening in the present, is to be aware of the characteristic features of the process. Such an understanding, if it can be achieved, may at least prevent us from making exaggerated claims for any radical model shifts.

It may be simplest and at the same time most useful to illustrate the process by an example. I propose to take one from the recent past, since one's understanding of the motives and actions of those involved in the process is likely to be fresh and accurate in the sense that it cannot be corrected or even influenced by the apparent wisdom of hindsight. The August 1975 issue of *The Architectural Review* carried a long article by Colin Rowe and Fred Koetter entitled

72 Imperial Rome, model at EVR, Rome

'Collage City'. Much of the piece was devoted to the decline and fall of the idea of utopia and in this connection drew attention in passing to Karl Popper's writings on utopianism and its dangers, one of the early occasions on which Popper's work appears to have exerted an influence on architectural criticism (the earliest and most notable contribution being probably Stanford Anderson's paper on tradition, read at the Architectural Association in 1963). The main theme of 'Collage City', however, was the notion of *bricolage*, a phrase borrowed from the French and particularly from the writings of Lévi-Strauss. *Bricolage*, the assembly of diverse elements which are at hand and which can be put together without the need to create new tools to fit some ultimate goal, is seen in some way as the reverse of so-called rational scientific action and also the reverse of utopian city planning aimed towards some known and fixed goal.

'The role of *bricolage*, which politics so much resembles and city planning surely should, is assumed as a saving and humanising influence which may prevent the catastrophes of the immediate past. The way in which *bricolage* would actually be applied on a day-to-day basis in the creation of the city would occur through adopting the methods of collage which Picasso and others had used effectively from the first decade of the century onwards.

'It is suggested that a collage approach, an approach in which objects (and attitudes) are conscripted or form out of their context, is – at the present day – the only way of dealing with the ultimate problems of either or both, Utopia and tradition, and the provenance of the architectural objects introduced into the social collage need not be of great consequence. It relates to taste and conviction. The objects can be aristocratic or they can be "folkish", academic or popular. Whether they originate in Pergamum or Dahomey, in Detroit or Dubrovnik, whether their implications are of the twentieth or the fifteenth century, need be of no great matter. Societies and persons assemble themselves according to their own interpretations of absolute reference and traditional value; and, up to a point, collage accommodates both hybrid display and the requirements of self-determination.'

73 Villa Adriana, Tivoli, AD 118– 138, model

The visual models which are actually invoked in the article are Imperial Rome and the Villa Adriana at Tivoli and seventeenth-century Rome; a photograph of a model reconstruction of Rome around the Colosseum is captioned as 'a perfect illustration of lavish bricolage' and a similar view of Hadrian's complex of buildings is used as a comparison with the single-mindedness of Versailles: 'While Versailles is a built version of one idea, the Villa Adriana at Tivoli is an accumulation of several ideas. The Villa Adriana presents the demands of the ideal and recognises at the same time the needs of the ad hoc. Here are the beginnings of collage.'

'Collage City' puts forward a prescription. It is a tentative, deliberately imprecise recipe in terms of how collage should be translated into late twentieth-century action. This is partly the case because such imprecision, such lack of rules, is part of the message, but it is also necessary in order to allow the written statements adequate latitude of architectural interpretation. In this sense, the models of reconstructions shown here also have the right degree of imprecision because they do not lend themselves to direct transfer into current usage.

Part of the argument is undoubtedly in favour of a model shift, and the chief attribute of the new model is that of collage. What is suggested is a kind of eclecticism, except that unlike its nineteenth-century version it is not a question of choosing between alternative models but almost simultaneously using a number of these; the new model is itself a plurality of possible models. This is perhaps a parallel to the idea of pluralism in society in general.

The choice of this alternative is clearly influenced by a criticism of what is seen to be the prevailing or at least recent mood: namely a desire to find definable simple goals to which buildings and planning in general should conform, and to which moreover it is thought they ought to conform if they are to be successful. How such conformity and such success are to be achieved is not clearly defined in the literature of the protagonists. A statement such as 'an all-embracing revolution of design would create a clean logic of social and biological relationships' (Sybil Moholy-Nagy, quoted in 'Collage City') represents only a state of mind and a certain wish but clearly not a prescription for an action with a known

96

outcome. In this sense, it conforms accurately to most architectural statements seeking alternatives.

But 'Collage City' is not only an intellectual criticism of architectural writings. It deplores the actual buildings and the town plans within which these are set. It certainly shares the prevailing public view that much of what is new has been a misfortune. Much of the criticism centres on an excessive simplicity of current building, on a lack of complexity when compared to older and more traditional examples. Part of this feeling may be due to the absence of decoration which Adolf Loos had advocated so strongly and largely successfully 67 years previously; part of it to the prevailing method of assembling buildings from very similar, perhaps even identical, elements by a simple and usually non-hierarchical additive process. *Bricolage*, on the contrary, assumes a very much greater variety of elements causing a more complex and possibly less ordered assembly. And this is clearly seen as being visually preferable. It could be said that Norman Foster used just such a form of *bricolage* with conspicuous success in the Hongkong and Shanghai Bank building completed in 1985.

The idea of *bricolage* and the example of Imperial Rome cannot, however, be said to be a logical extension of any argument in favour of complexity. Other methods and other historical examples could be equally appropriate. The choice of this particular answer is, one suspects, influenced by visual preferences which are already in existence, however tentatively. To put it another way, a visual model has already been sensed which to some extent at least answers the verbally defined criticisms.

Something slightly similar was suggested in an earlier book by Charles Jencks and Nathan Silver, *Adhocism: the Case of Improvisation*, as Nathan Silver was quick to point out rather bitterly in a letter to the *Architectural Review* published in October 1975. Charles Jencks followed this up with a more carefully argued letter in the November issue, suggesting that many of the ideas and examples which had been put forward by him and Silver as well as those by Rowe and Koetter were in the air during the 1960s, 'were one part of the modern movements in architecture . . .'. In the same issue, Reyner Banham attempted to ascribe these notions to the frequent articles on townscape which had appeared in the *Architectural Review* much earlier, and especially to one by Ivor de Wolfe in December 1949 which rooted these ideas in the Picturesque Movement of the eighteenth century and the writings of Sir Uvedale Price.

A more serious precursor than *Adhocism* was Robert Venturi's controversial and highly influential book *Complexity and Contradiction in Architecture*. This was illustrated by a large number of small photographs of buildings from the past and the present, a

74 Norman Foster (Foster Associates)
Hong Kong and Shanghai Bank, Hong Kong, 1982–85

great many of which hinted at complex assemblies of parts. The accumulation of visual references suggested an alternative architectural stream in which there is a considerable emphasis on Baroque and Rococo examples, and on Lutyens and Alvar Aalto from the more immediate past. Moreover, the resemblance between many of Aalto's characteristic features – the control of light, the use of curvilinear forms, the separation between the inner and outer layers of a building – and those of typical Baroque and Rococo buildings can often be traced without great difficulty. But perhaps equally crucial to Venturi's theme, and especially to the influence which it was able to exert, was the fact that at the end of the book he was able to include illustrations of his

75 Alvar Aalto
Church at Vuoksenniska (Imatra),
1956–59

76 *Venturi and Short
House for Mrs Venturi, Chestnut
Hill, Penn. 1962–64*

own work, some of which could be seen to be carrying out in architectural forms the issues which had been raised in the text and which had been illustrated in the margin with only historical references. This was particularly true of Venturi's house for his mother in Chestnut Hill, Pennsylvania, of 1962. A comparison between the entrance side of the house and a postcard view of the present state of the Portico di Ottavia in Rome, built in AD 147, suggests not only some of the historical allusions but also a certain non-conformist attitude to design and to assemblage. (Nor is the comparison fortuitous: the postcard was sent to me from Rome in 1966 by Venturi.) In other words, it was possible to demonstrate that the verbal theme was viable.

Venturi's verbal theme could also be said to have visual analogies, not only with Rome but with the much closer at hand Shingle Style of the East Coast of the USA. It was a style strongly evident in domestic architecture from the early 1870s to the late 1880s and was most often seen at the seaside towns of Rhode Island, Massachusetts and Maine, where this blending of the classical American Colonial tradition with Queen Anne influences from England and some Japanese elements seen in recently published books seems appropriately casual; it had a certain whimsy that was right for a holiday house.

Whether those who read Venturi's book in the years after its publication liked or disliked his buildings was not immediately relevant, nor did it necessarily affect the impact of the argument. Its main themes stemmed again from a criticism of the view and practices which were dominant in the late 1950s and early 1960s. Venturi strongly felt that the mainstream of modern architecture had taken the easy road by neglecting a whole range of problems and had in the process impoverished itself, had become banal; that what was required was 'the difficult unity through inclusion rather than the easy unity through exclusion'. Many of the ideas of ambiguity and contradiction which Venturi valued in architecture, as William Empson had valued them in literature, could be summed up in a phrase which he borrowed from a discussion of Donne's poetry in *The Well Wrought Urn* by Cleanth Brooks, the notion of 'the tradition of both–and'. This is seen as the reverse of the established view, the tradition of 'either–or'

77 *Portico di Ottavia, Rome, AD
147 (postcard)*

100

that has characterised modern architecture: 'a sun screen is probably nothing else; a support is seldom an enclosure; a wall is not violated by window penetrations but is totally interrupted by glass; programme functions are exaggeratedly articulated into wings or segregated space pavilions . . . Such manifestations of articulation and clarity are foreign to an architecture of complexity and contradiction, which tends to include "both–and" rather than exclude "either–or".'

It was possible to agree with Venturi's criticism of much of modern architecture, and also to subscribe to his prescriptions for an alternative course of action which had ample historical precedent, without necessarily assuming that the outcome of such an alternative attitude would produce buildings similar to those by the Venturi office. But the fact that such buildings existed and could be seen to be different from those based on earlier – and at that time more orthodox – assumptions provided some assurance that visual forms could be evolved from these arguments, and that they need not be simple copies of old models; that we were dealing with ideas which were buildable, just as Rowe and Koetter's choice of Imperial Rome tried to show that some buildable form could be related to their arguments. This I believe to be extremely important to any discussion of architecture.

Ideas which were often not dissimilar to these had been discussed by Aldo van Eyck in the pages of *Forum*, a magazine published in Holland, and had also been given a built form in van Eyck's Municipal Orphanage School on the edge of Amsterdam of 1957–60, which soon became a place of architectural pilgrimage. Much of van Eyck's architecture tried to celebrate and emphasise apparently simple functions by visually complex means, and continues to do so as in his Mothers' House in Amsterdam completed in 1980, or in the pavilions for the Padua Psychiatric Hospital in Bockel and the additions to the European Space Research and Technology Centre in Noordwijk, Holland, published in 1990. His attitude towards architecture had been considerably affected by the buildings and way of life of the Dogon in West Africa. They perhaps provided the source for a model shift in much the same way that Mannerist buildings provided clues to Venturi.

78 Peabody and Stearns 'Kragsyde' (G. N. Black House), Manchester-by-the-Sea, Mass. 1882–83

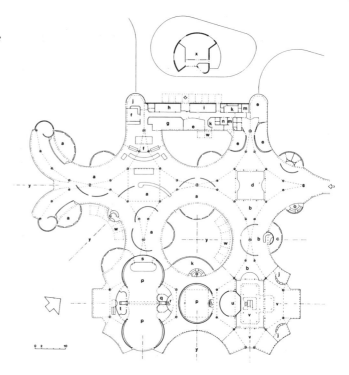

My attempt to describe a single article in a
prominent architectural magazine and then to trace
some of its antecedents may appear as part of some
art-historical game of attributing sources and estab-
lishing claims of priority. It is not intended to be that.
What I am anxious to show is that when a particular
set of answers is seen to be failing in some way or
other – formally, socially, technically – the amount
and intensity of criticism increases; certain aspects
begin to be singled out and are seen to be responsible
for the dominant failings. As a result, alternative
suggestions are first made and then tentative answers
provided, usually by going through the process of
making a model shift, and these in turn are
elaborated and criticised. What I am attempting to do
is to describe a particular and recent instance of the P_1
$\rightarrow$ TT $\rightarrow$ EE $\rightarrow$ P_2 sequence, or more precisely its
fuller version which takes account of the multiplicity
of trials:

$$P_1 \rightarrow \begin{matrix} TS_1 \\ TS_2 \\ \vdots \\ TS_n \end{matrix} \rightarrow EE \rightarrow P_2$$

where P_1 stands for the original problem, TS for the tentative solutions, EE for error-elimination and P_2 for the problem which is likely to emerge as requiring an answer as a result of the acceptance of the new theory.

The existence of an emergent problem is often seen in the process of criticism itself or as soon as a tentative solution is proposed. The Editors of the *Architectural Review*, in a leader which preceded the article on 'Collage City', felt it important to note that:

'Colin Rowe takes the view that the Western City is above all a compact of small realisations and incompleted purposes. Though there are self-contained architectural set pieces, like the plums in a pudding, which create small homogeneous environments, the overall picture is one in which architectural intentions constantly "collide" and he suggests that we should learn to take more pleasure in this wholesome fact of architectural experience than as yet we do.

'The only rider that we would wish to add to this doctrine is that there are certain "collisions" which, as it were, enhance the mutually colliding parties and others which destroy them. Modern practice, with its exaggerated disconcern for the pre-existing, has given rise to too much of the destructive sort of collision. For fruitful collisions, there must be among architects a revival of the topographic sense.'

Nor has the particular line of criticism and of tentative solutions which I have traced been the only alternative, even among architects working within the relatively circumscribed area of the East Coast of the USA. A group which has been labelled 'The New York Five' has been teaching and practising from the early 1960s onwards, basing its work on the assumption that the principles of cubism and the enormously suggestive buildings of Le Corbusier provide a storehouse of design ideas which has been far from fully explored. Their argument would be that we need a shift to a model of the recent past which was abandoned prematurely and needlessly. Colin Rowe, Robert and Denise Venturi and the 'Five' (Peter Eisenman, Michael Graves, Charles Gwathmy, John Hejduk and Richard Meier) all know each other and are familiar with each other's work and writings. This is not therefore a case of alternatives being

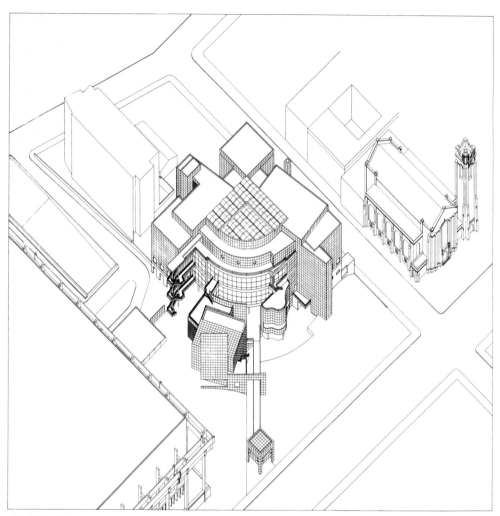

80 Richard Meier
The High Museum, Atlanta,
Georgia, 1980–83

worked out in isolation, but rather a number of deliberate probings to find tentative solutions to what are seen as the current problems of architecture.

Other groups or individuals are looking for still different alternatives elsewhere; the series TS_1, TS_2, TS_3 . . . is always difficult to define. A close look at any period of history will reveal a wider range of solutions than is normally assumed to be the case from the stylistic label which the period carries. This does not deny the fact that a particular type of solution may become dominant and exert the force of a paradigm in Thomas Kuhn's sense. However, we must also recognise that what one of the current

104

alternatives proposes is that such a paradigm should be avoided, that there is a virtue in a plurality of sources and that the model should be the absence of a single model. This does not in itself suggest a state of scepticism nor a position which should necessarily be strenuously avoided.

Something similar, it has been suggested, occurs in science. 'It is difficult, for instance, to find any lengthy period in the history of any science in the last 300 years when the Kuhnian picture of "normal science" prevails. What seems to be far more common is for scientific disciplines to involve a variety of co-present research approaches (traditions).'

Because the absence of a readily copiable precedent makes architectural design extremely difficult, it may well be that the success of collage has been less general than its advocates hoped. Its freedom and emphasis on plurality may have weakened its everyday usefulness. What has instead become much more pervasive is a practice of modulating an architecture out of the classical tradition by treating its elements freely, occasionally wittily, often with deliberate exaggeration as in Mannerism. Arguably it is a kind of collage but from a familiar, limited and readily usable set of components. The style is now so widespread and recognisable that it has been possible to label it with the not very descriptive or helpful title of 'postmodernism', a description used in literary criticism.

Running parallel with the spread of postmodernism has been a single-minded and important exploration of making buildings from industrially produced

81 Charles Moore and Robert L Harper
Williams College Museum of Art, Williamstown, Mass. 1983

82 Pierre Chareau (with Bernard Bijvoet)
Maison de Verre, Paris, 1928–32 main staircase

*83 Dave King and Rod McAlister
School of Architecture and Building
Engineering, University of
Liverpool, 1988
link bridge*

*84 Edward Cullinan Architects
Uplands Conference Centre, High
Wycombe, 1982–84
seating area*

parts, an evolution of the arguments of the machine aesthetic, but with a strong emphasis on the products of a more recent and more sophisticated technology. It should however again be recognised that much of this search, which extends to furniture and industrial design, is strongly influenced by visual preferences rather than simple engineering principles. It has also produced a set of recognisable characteristics which are subsumed under the stylistic label of 'high-tech'. The argument again, as in the 1920s and 1930s, is that a new technology provides great opportunities which it is vital for architects to understand and apply. The appropriate technology is now seen to derive not from ocean liners or motor cars but from space exploration and offshore oil rigs.

Yet another stream can be discerned in the concern for solutions appropriate to the given context, a belief in a kind of architectural regionalism which is often allied to a deliberate use of much lower levels of technology, even a return to an arts and crafts tradition. Economic stringency and the state of the building industry in most countries make such solutions frequently more feasible as well as publicly acceptable. Like postmodernism or high-tech, the style is not confined to a particular country but is sufficiently widespread to have acquired the title of 'regional pragmatism'. Despite its belief in pragmatic solutions there is sufficient coherence in the formal solutions for a stylistic grouping to be possible, although, some of its proponents might claim, not necessarily desirable.

As in the case of postmodernism, literary thought has more recently given us the term 'deconstruction', yet another trend in architectural exploration. Somewhat as in literary criticism, deconstruction in architecture gives emphasis to the separateness, perhaps even to the autonomy, of the constituent elements on the assumption that each has a meaning which needs to be revealed. The methods of literary criticism are not immediately applicable to design, however, since architecture has to be created before its parts can be analysed. For its formal images deconstructivism has, perhaps paradoxically, gone to the art and architecture which was briefly developed in the Soviet Union in the 1920s, to constructivism in fact, in order to have a model from which to start. Much of constructivism emphasised the abstract as

106

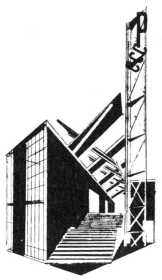

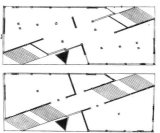

85 K Melnikov
USSR Pavilion, International
Exposition of Decorative Art, Paris,
1925

well as the kinetic – or at least the apparently kinetic –
and frequently produced visually complex forms.
Much deconstructive architecture has similar aims.

Whether one of the known tentative solutions
eventually becomes dominant or some quite different
approach establishes itself, or whether we cease to
have a well-entrenched paradigm for a considerable
time, does not affect the argument about the process
of change. This is simply that in architecture, and
probably all the visual arts, the sequence which Karl
Popper suggested for science ($P_1 \rightarrow TS \rightarrow EE \rightarrow P_2$)
generally holds good, providing us with the clearest
understanding of a process which probably goes on
continually and from time to time erupts to create
major shifts.

86 COOP Himmelblau
Hot Flat, project, 1978–

13

The emergence from time to time of a solution which becomes common currency and which may be the result of a major shift, giving its label to an epoch, should not obscure the fact that at most times a variety of answers occurs simultaneously, as suggested in the preceding section. This is especially true during periods of transition. When a dominant solution emerges, when it becomes sufficiently accepted and its examples sufficiently numerous, we in a sense see the development of a new tradition. Often, however, a number of traditions are in use at the same time, for it is very rare for only one kind of tentative answer to be put forward. It is perhaps only the need for history books to simplify and abstract which creates the impression that a stylistic conquest has occurred, leaving the tradition victorious and the remainder totally vanquished.

In order to try and combat this view it may be useful to look at a single volume of *Wasmuth*, an important and respected publication produced in Berlin by a publishing house which is best remembered for its early recognition of the work of Frank Lloyd Wright in 1910 and 1911. *Wasmuth* lends itself particularly well to such an analysis because its coverage was genuinely international and because it did not adopt a polemical position which would have made it select only a narrow category of buildings. Naturally it had to apply certain criteria of selection, which are evident not least in the emphasis given to German examples. But since a great deal of the work of that period which was later to find its way into the history books was done in Germany, this is not a hindrance. Like most architectural magazines *Wasmuth* moreover dealt with only a small part of the built environment since it only published the work of architects. Traditions which affected a wide range of building activity therefore remained unrecorded in its pages.

The year 1927 has been chosen for reasons which are partly fortuitous, but which are mainly due to the fact that a number of architectural events which were subsequently seen as important can be ascribed to this year. In Germany, the Deutscher Werkbund organised a housing exhibition at Weissenhof, a

87 Le Corbusier
Villa at Garches, 1927
drive and entrance

88 Le Corbusier
League of Nations, Geneva,
competition project, 1927

suburb of Stuttgart, which was directed by Mies van der Rohe and which contained buildings by Le Corbusier, J. J. P. Oud, Mart Stam and a number of German architects who apart from Mies included Peter Behrens, Walter Gropius, Ludwig Hilberseimer, Hans Poelzig, Hans Scharoun, Bruno Taut and Max Taut. In France Le Corbusier's house at Garches dates from this year; in Switzerland a competition was held for the design of the League of Nations Building in Geneva and Le Corbusier's entry was rejected on allegedly technical grounds; a more radical solution by Hannes Meyer and Hans Wittwer was also discarded; in Finland Alvar Aalto was successful in the competition for the design of the Municipal Library at Viipuri, although its building did not start for some years; in the Soviet Union Melnikov had built the Rusakov Club in Moscow and Leonidov designed the remarkable project for the Lenin Institute; in the USA Frank Lloyd Wright had just built the Ocotillo Desert Camp near Chandler, Arizona, while he was working on the San Marcos-in-the-Desert project. (Wright had started Taliesin III at Spring Green, Wisconsin, two years earlier and Walter Gropius had finished the Bauhaus at Dessau in 1926.)

It can therefore safely be said that by the year 1927 the new architecture of the 1920s – what was later to be described as the International Style (except for the work of Wright) – had achieved a certain footing in a number of countries. However, the 1927 volume of *Wasmuth* shows that this particular style was not the only alternative which was being explored, and that

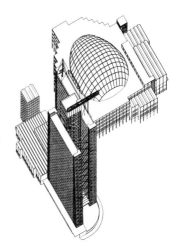

89 Hannes Meyer and Hans Wittwer
League of Nations, Geneva,
competition project, 1927

90 Ivan Leonidov
Lenin Institute, project, 1927

91 Frank Lloyd Wright
San Marcos-in-the-Desert, near
Chandler, Arizona, project, 1927

earlier explorations were still being pushed in novel directions.

The 1927 volume of *Wasmuth's Monatshefte für Baukunst* contains 1428 illustrations which cover work in Austria, Belgium, Czechoslovakia, Denmark, Germany, Finland, France, Galicia, Greece, Holland, Hungary, Italy, Japan (one entry), Yugoslavia, Poland, Russia, Spain, Sweden, Switzerland, Tunisia and the USA. It clearly sets out to record what were considered significant buildings throughout the world.

The results of the competition for new buildings for the League of Nations in Geneva are shown and described in more than one issue and obviously aroused a good deal of interest. The first illustration is of a highly classical prize-winning entry by Erik zu Politz with Klophaus and Schoch from Hamburg; it is immediately followed by a submission which consists of a sphere with adjacent minarets designed by Peter Birkenholz of Munich. Another prize-winning design illustrated in the same month was a romantic classical project by the Roman architect Giuseppe Vago. No stylistic thread can be readily distinguished in that group.

A subsequent issue shows the axonometric and traffic circulation plan of the Hannes Meyer design, drawings which emphasise the radical and functionalist aspects of the scheme. In contrast, the elevation

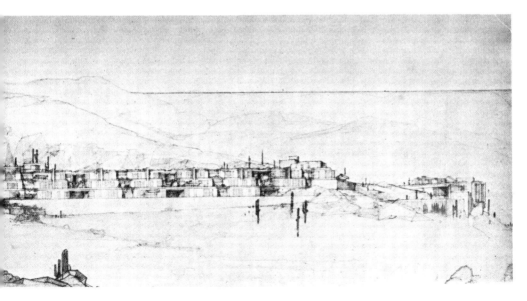

of Le Corbusier's buildings in their setting convey much more the poetic aspirations of modern architecture. These illustrations are followed by another prize-winning entry, a finger plan by Nils Eriksson in that simplified and adapted classical style which was much in evidence in Sweden, particularly up to the Stockholm Exhibition of 1930.

The other projects chosen for illustration throughout that year show a similar variety, as well as a similar spread between those whose names are well remembered and those now unknown. The first group includes a design for a hotel by J. J. P. Oud in Brno, Czechoslovakia, the town where later Bata was to build important examples of modern industrial architecture and Mies was to design the Tugendhat house in 1930. Other international style buildings are a house in Frankfurt by Ernst May and a project for a gas plant by Guiseppe Terragni. Mies van der Rohe on the other hand is represented by a traditional house at Neubabelsberg near Berlin (where Erich Mendelsohn had completed the Einstein Tower in 1921) with a neo-classical shuttered front, credited to him and Werner von Walthausen, which dates from 1914. The influence of Schinkel is still very obvious.

The house, illustrated as part of a discussion on flat and pitched roofs, is quite different from the project for a brick house of 1922, with its apparently exploding planes reaching out into the garden, or the block of flats which was going up for the Weissenhof Siedlung in 1927. In another issue there is a block of flats in Vienna by Josef Hoffman which sits uneasily between neo-classicism and the international style. It has extremely taut planes punctured by windows and tall arcades in a manner which sixty years later we associate with the work of Aldo Rossi. This extensive range of stylistic answers by those architects whose work is seen as crucial to the development of twentieth-century architecture suggests that perhaps at any time, and certainly in a period of transition, choices may be modified for different conditions and no simple answer is ever inevitable.

95 J J P Oud
Hotel Stiassni, Brno, project, 1926

Less well-known names include Theodor Lammers, who was represented by a school in Oostzaan near Amsterdam; this was a spirited continuation of the work of Michael de Klerk, who had died in 1923, and demonstrated a markedly different strand of twentieth-century architecture from that embodied in the work of Ernst May or J. J. P. Oud. Yet another strand was evident in a house in Phoenix, Arizona, by Albert Chase McArthur, a Harvard-trained American architect who had been highly influenced by Frank Lloyd Wright and was at one time his pupil and then his collaborator.

Nor had the eighteenth-century tradition of neo-classicism and its later reworking died out. An

96 Guiseppe Terragni
Gasworks, Como, project, 1927

113

97 Mies van der Rohe, Werner von
Walthausen
Haus Urbig, Neubabelsberg, 1914

appraisal by Stein Eiler Rasmussen discusses two
state schools at Randers and Viborg in Denmark, by
H. Kampmann and C. Kampmann. Many of the
simple, ordered attributes of those buildings, as well
as the drawing techniques used, were current at the
Royal Academy in Copenhagen at that time and are
clearly visible in a design by Kay Agertoft, one of a
number of projects from students at the school
illustrated in that issue. The editors also use a set of
drawings made by Arne Jacobsen while a student at

98 Josef Hoffman
Flats, Felix Mottlstrasse, Vienna

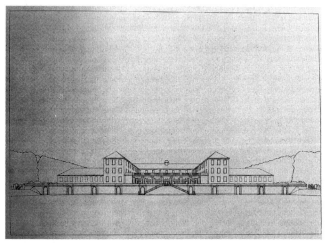

100 H and C Kampmann
School, Viborg, Jutland, 1918–20

99 T. Lammers
ʾchool, Oostzaan

101 H and C Kampmann
School, Randers, Jutland

the Academy in 1925, as an example of the simplicity and 'objectivity' (Sachlichkeit) which the magazine wanted to record. What is of equal interest in retrospect is the degree to which that design already embodies so many of the characteristics which Jacobsen was to deploy throughout his architectural career.

The polemical theme which recurs throughout the year centres on the argument as to whether flat or pitched roofs are appropriate; it is about style, but

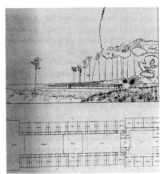

102 Kay Agertoft
Holiday Homes, Student project at
the Academy of Fine Arts,
Copenhagen, 1925

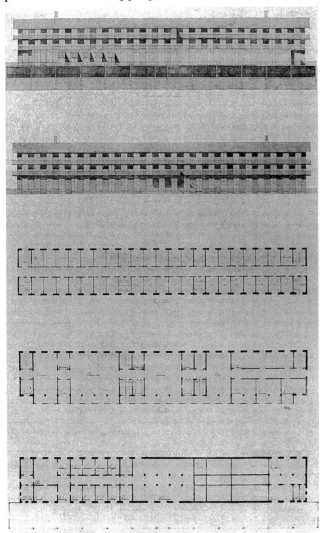

103 Arne Jacobsen
Bathing Resort, Student project at
the Academy of Fine Arts,
Copenhagen, 1925

*104 Paul Schultze-Naumburg
Haus Rhodius, Burgbrohl (Eifel)*

practicality, cost, technology and nationalism are all invoked. The argument was also conducted in other magazines, notably by Walter Gropius in *Bauwelt* and by others in the *Deutsche Bauzeitung*. In an important and extended article by Werner Hegemann, 'Artistic questions of the day regarding the building of single family houses', comparisons are made between the work of Paul Schultze-Naumburg, whose villas resembled some of the later and more formal houses of Lutyens, and that of Ernst May, best known for his extensive settlements while City Architect of Frankfurt-am-Main between 1925 and 1930. The author takes Schultze-Naumburg to task for attempting racial arguments that pitched roofs belong to the north German tradition while flat roofs were 'unGerman' and had their origin in the south or Middle East. This is dismissed by Hegemann as irrelevant and countered by the statement of an engineer in Haifa, quoted in the Gropius survey, that in Palestine it was generally acknowledged that flat roofs could not be made waterproof. The prime virtue of the pitched roof is thought to be the very long experience we have of its construction.

Behind this discussion for and against a particular building form lies a deeper argument about whether or not we are to put aside history and the lessons it has produced. Hegemann suggests that on his own admission Ernst May has turned his back on the past. The error of such a move is explained by Hegemann through a linguistic analogy: just because there are contemporary concepts for which no German word is available there is no need to use international words such as radio, telephone or aeroplane. German words, he claims, such as 'Fernsprecher', 'Funkspruch' or 'Flugzeug' can be developed from the existing language. There may be a further reason for neglecting the past: it has no lessons to teach because form itself is considered irrelevant. A supporter of Ernst May is quoted as saying 'this house is not a problem of form but a shell in accordance with biological necessities'. We are back to the assumptions of Semper and the pitfalls of the biological analogy.

Werner Hegemann tries to show that the May villa under discussion is not really as 'objective', as free of formal problems, as its architect might suggest. Perhaps his ultimate argument rests on the fact that

*105 Ernst May
House, Frankfurt-Ginnheim*

116

'the arts, however, of which architecture is the queen, are only preoccupied with form. A house which is not a problem of form cannot be considered as art, and the presumption that such a house could in a meaningful sense be poetic will one day appear as the misconception of a temporary fashion.'

14

If the suggestions describing the process of change are accepted as having at least some validity, two questions immediately arise: who performs the criticism which is required for a problem to be recognised and thus starts the sequence which may lead to different solutions, and what determines the severity of that criticism and the extent of any resulting model shift?

Architecture does not exist in isolation, either in its attempt to recognise problems or in its efforts to produce solutions; it is influenced by events outside itself. For example, the literature of the nineteenth century is full of references to the horrors of the city, both as a social phenomenon and as a visual effect. Much of the emphasis is on its unnaturalness, on what Dickens described in *Dombey and Son* as 'being like a monster!' Dickens also saw the city and its way of life as causing the major disasters inherent in his society. Writing in *The Examiner* in 1848, he declares: 'Drunkenness, as a national horror, is the effect of many causes. Foul smells, disgusting habitations, bad workshops and workshop customs; want of light, air and water, the absence of all easy means of decency and health, are commonest among its common, every day, physical causes'. The writings of Charles Dickens have been successfully analysed for their frequent references to the city and all the ills ascribed to it in the middle of the nineteenth century, as well as for the virtues which were seen as leading to happiness. In *Sketches of Young Couples*, published in 1840, Dickens advises his readers to 'learn to centre all their hopes of real and lasting happiness in their own fire side, let them cherish the faith that in home, and all the English virtues which love of home engenders, lies the only true source of domestic felicity; let them believe that round the household gods, contentment and tranquility cluster in their gentlest and most graceful forms; and that many weary hunters of happiness through the noisy world, have learnt this truth too late and found a cheerful spirit and a quiet mind only at home at last!' It is a recipe which, with the possible emendation of gods into goods, has had a profound effect; coupled with the bitter moral criticism of the city, it can be seen to

106 *Back Yards, Islington, London*

have direct and strong effects on architectural and planning ideas.

In a similar way, literature and particularly poetry which concentrated on the idyllic rural scene and often equated a purer, better past with an arcadian idyll, as in Oliver Goldsmith's 'The Deserted Village' (1770), surely helped to create points of view which had an effect outside the world of literature and can be paralleled with notions in architecture and planning. American writing displayed very much the same traits as that in England; if anything, the anti-urban lobby was even stronger. The history of 'the intellectual versus the city' has been admirably charted by Morton and Lucia White in a book of that name, from the early writings of Thomas Jefferson to Frank Lloyd Wright's attack and his alternative, Broadacre City. Jefferson epitomised at the beginnings of the history of the United States an ambivalence between a desire to live the virtuous existence and the reluctant recognition that cities may be an economic necessity, especially if the country were to achieve any kind of economic independence; the ambivalence has remained to this day. Attacks and commendations of this kind eventually have their effect and spill over into the world of action, especially when other forces – those of public health, land economics or population growth – enormously reinforce such widely held literary views. These become the general intellectual climate within which architecture functions.

Neither Goldsmith's evocation of 'Sweet Auburn, loveliest village of the plain', fast being depopulated, nor Jefferson's hard sentiment, expressed thirty years later, 'I view great cities as pestilential to the morals, the health and the liberties of man' (from which he subsequently somewhat relented, however), determined urban forms. Wright's Broadacre City, Le Corbusier's Ville Contemporaine and garden cities such as Raymond Unwin's Letchworth could all be said to be answers to the criticisms levelled at the nineteenth-century city, yet the organisation and the visual effects of these three tentative solutions are widely different. Architectural forms are not predetermined by the inital criticism, and the choice of forms remains open within a wide spectrum. Other layers of criticism are superimposed, many of which stem not from social or economic or intellectual

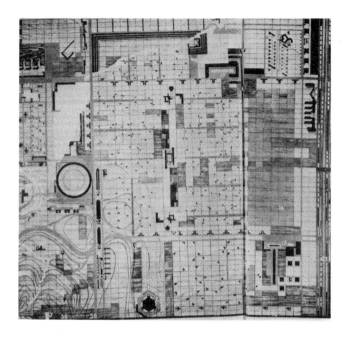

107 Frank Lloyd Wright
*Broadacre City, model by Taliesin
Fellowship, 1932*

standpoints but from formal, visual criteria; inevitably certain aspects of criticism always arise from architectural considerations, in particular from a dissatisfaction with some elements of the architecture of the immediately preceding period.

Public discussion of general issues helps to direct architectural thinking into definite channels, and the desire to achieve a solution of such general problems also creates the building opportunities which are essential if architectural projects are to become reality. The notion that a particular kind of reality might exist and might indeed be an answer to some

108 Le Corbusier
Ville Contemporaine, 1922

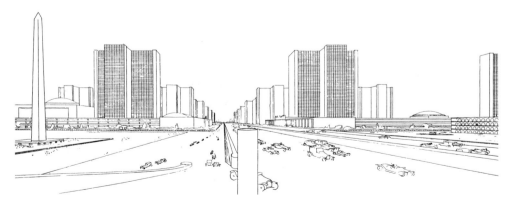

120

of these issues is often suggested, moreover, by projects or writings which point in a recognisable direction. Neither Broadacre City nor Ville Contemporaine exist in the form in which they were conceived, but many of their elements have been appropriated by others; they have found their way, however diluted, into the currency both of general and of architectural ideas. Letchworth exists, but Letchworth itself depends on the writings and diagrams of Ebenezer Howard's *Tomorrow: a Peaceful Path to Real Reform*, first published in 1898 under that title and re-issued in 1902 as *Garden Cities of Tomorrow*. The memorandum of association of the First Garden City Ltd stated clearly that its object was:

'To promote and further the distribution of the industrial population upon the land upon the lines suggested in Mr Ebenezer Howard's book entitled *Garden Cities of Tomorrow* . . . and to form a garden city, (that is to say) a town or settlement for agricultural, industrial, commercial and residential purposes or any of them in accordance with Mr Howard's scheme or any modification thereof'.

Its prospectus said that:

'The *root* idea of Mr Howard's book is to deal at once with the two vital questions of *overcrowding* in our towns and the *depopulation* of our rural districts, and to thereby reduce the congestion of population of great towns, or at least arrest progress.'

The existence of Letchworth in turn inspired other projects, though many adopted its visual patterns (especially Unwin's view of garden city development as consisting of 'twelve houses to the acre', which he popularised in *Nothing Gained by Overcrowding* published in 1912) without taking over its social and economic policies. Garden cities often became garden suburbs; once achieved, the visual form was more readily transferable than its underlying assumptions. It was a pattern which could be used with great ease and which found its way into the inter-war suburban estates of Britain and the post-war new towns. It could also be seen in the great suburban developments of the United States which were clearly influenced by earlier American designs, such as the layouts of Fredrick Law Olmsted. Although Olmsted is now best remembered for Central Park, New York,

121

and occasionally for his successful campaign to save and preserve Niagara Falls, he was, with Calvert Vaux, also greatly involved in the design of housing layouts; Riverside, Illinois (1869) has all the suburban elements with which we have become familiar in the succeeding hundred years.

Ebenezer Howard probably knew some of these developments in the United States. He first went there in 1871 at the age of 21 and started farming in Nebraska. Soon afterwards, however, he went to Chicago where he stayed until 1876. He revisited the States once or twice in his life. Chicago in the early 1870s was a remarkable city of intellectual ferment as

109 Olmsted, Vaux and Co
General plan of Riverside, Ill., 1869

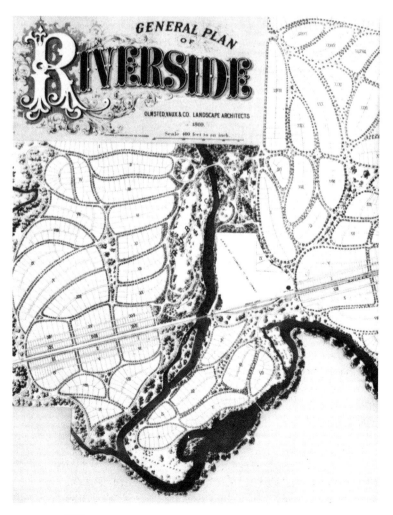

well as phenomenal building activity where the layout of an area such as that at Riverside, just to the west of the edge of the city, was only a small part of the total building programme. Howard's proposals stem, however, principally from social and political ideals which he found expressed in Edward Bellamy's utopian novel *Looking Backward*. This highly popular book came out in America in 1888 and a year later in London. Howard did not derive the garden city in any of its formal senses from Bellamy's novel, but was moved by an optimistic vision of an utopian Boston in the year 2000, which in turn was part of the nineteenth-century concern for and criticism of the social, economic, moral and physical problems of the city.

The ways in which general ideas and building action are enmeshed thus become visible on even a simple examination; a closer look would undoubtedly reveal greater intricacies and probably a more continuous interaction. What I believe would not be demonstrated on even the closest analysis is that built forms are in some precise way determined by the general notions of any period, or that it could ever be shown that architects have no formal choices. Very often there is a plurality of general ideas which may even be in conflict, and architects will reinforce visual predilections by supporting them with deliberately selected social notions.

The legacy of Letchworth, for instance, did not remain uncriticised. When the New Towns built around London in the post-war period were beginning to be rather more than building sites, a great deal of criticism was levelled at their appearance, particularly at their diffuse nature and their total lack of urbanity and sense of place. This attack was reinforced by some of the findings of sociologists who had registered dissatisfaction with the arrangements of the New Towns, especially by housewives, and who had labelled this malaise as 'New Town blues'. A visual dislike found an apparent social rationale and the later New Towns (Cumbernauld, Runcorn and the unbuilt project for Hook) tried to produce denser, more obviously urban answers.

Others who favoured low-density suburban development argued for it as a popular form which, if the private market was any indication of preference, was much closer to public demand than any dense

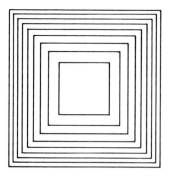

110 *Fresnel square*
Each successive annular ring
diminishes in width but has exactly
the same area as its predecessor; the
outer band has therefore exactly the
same area as the middle square

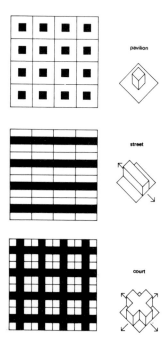

111 *Leslie Martin and Lionel March*
Pavilion, street and court diagrams

urban arrangement, and could also find sociological writings to support them. Herbert Gans's study of 'Levittowners' between 1958 and 1962 showed that the people of this suburban community in New Jersey liked being where they were and that their community life depended not on density or planning, but on 'the population mix they encounter' and very much on the values they brought with them. He found that 'most new suburbanites are pleased with the community that develops; they enjoy their house and outdoor living and take pleasure from the large supply of compatible people, without experiencing the boredom or malaise ascribed to suburban homogeneity'.

Such sociological findings tended to be bolstered by later geometric studies which cast grave doubts on the efficiency of certain forms of high-density housing in terms of land use. Those by Leslie Martin and Lionel March which appeared from 1966 onwards compared pavilion, linear and courtyard layouts and were able to demonstrate the efficiency of built form organised around hollow squares. Lionel March went on in 1967 to extend these diagrams to the layout of towns and to argue for 'a free house development along a network of routes' fairly close to the sort of semi-suburban development that can be found in many parts of the United States. Lionel March was enormously influenced by the writings and projects of Frank Lloyd Wright and found such areas as Bucks County near Philadelphia in some points analogous to Broadacre City. His mathematical analysis of building forms, routes and densities was motivated by a clear preference for certain physical arrangements; the selection of the aspects to be studied stemmed initially from an architectural bias.

These criticisms and the suggestions made by March have to some extent been put into practice. The efficiency of layouts based on the relation of areas which can be found in Fresnel squares has been applied in large-scale housing projects in Britain, particularly by David Lea and Richard McCormack both of whom were influenced by March at Cambridge. The demand for some kind of urbanity – often more in the minds of architects than of householders – has taken various forms. Extreme positions can be found in Aldo Rossi's housing in the Gallaratese 2 complex in Milan of 1969–73, carried out in a monumental neo-classical tradition, or in the idiosyn-cratic designs of Bofill at Saint-Quentin-en-Yvelines near Paris where housing is agglomerated into a latter-day palace form. The much more frequent answer has been to think of a small market town. This makes possible a measure of density in one of two forms: either a slightly heightened variant of cottage architecture or a modified version of eight-eenth-century terrace housing, both of which have strong popular appeal.

What such continuous interaction suggests is that the move from P_1 to P_2 can often be quite rapid and that an essential element of the process is that there is rarely a natural position at which it comes to an end. In order to emphasise this continuity, it might be appropriate to re-write Popper's sequence as:

$$\ldots \text{general criticism} \to P_n \to \overset{\nearrow \; TS_1 \; \searrow}{\underset{\searrow \; TS_3 \; \nearrow}{TS_2}} \to EE \to P_{n+1} \to \text{general criticism}$$

where 'general criticism' deals dominantly with questions outside architecture and the sequence P_n to P_{n+1} with primarily architectural matters; TS is influenced by knowledge at time t.

Foreground

15

The second of the questions put at the beginning of the last section – what determines the severity of criticisim and thus the extent of any model shift? – brings discussion close to the problems of designing a building and therefore also to the attitudes of the architect involved. For it is only through the building itself that the nature of the criticism becomes evident and can sensibly be assessed. Criticism in this case does not imply the kind of critical analysis which may occur in a verbal assessment, but the specific problem definition, arising out of criticism, which becomes the guide to subsequent action. Part of this definition may indeed be non-verbal. In this instance, moreover, any action must take an architectural form because the problems which it tries to resolve are architectural; their origin may have been social or economic or technical, but eventually they have to be stated in a way which can reasonably be resolved in terms of buildings. If that is not so, the attempts at resolution are likely to be futile. This is so obvious that it should not need to be stated, yet architects are frequently asked to solve problems entirely outside their domain and as often as not believe that they can do so. New housing, for example, will do nothing to resolve the problems of poverty – indeed it may add to them – yet we often act as if it did, and by doing so fail as a society to take other important, and possibly more useful, remedial action.

At this point, I believe, it is also important to distinguish clearly between three aspects which are inevitably part of any architectural problem. The *first* of these relates to those parts which can be taken as given. At any one time and in any particular place, a range of building materials exists and is equally available to all. If financial restrictions reduce that range, any given restriction limits that range equally for all concerned. These materials are assembled by methods which are in current usage. Both the materials and the methods of construction are subject to certain physical laws – the force of gravity, the strength of materials, chemical action such as oxidation – and in any locality to legal restrictions governing safety, public health etc. Further, locally or nationally enacted legal limitations may affect the placement, shape and purpose of buildings through planning legislation and its associated ordinances. These again apply equally to all in any particular situation, although sectors such as government construction may at times be exempt. The present state of technology and the current legal requirements which surround practice can therefore be taken as given elements and, within reason, as unavoidable starting points.

The established stock of buildings also belongs to the category of given elements. In the awareness of any person, the number of buildings that exist is undoubtedly going to be greater than the amount to be added through solving any particular architectural task; it is extremely hard to imagine anyone creating more buildings than that person knew previously. Such architectural innocence is moreover inconceivable at any time in history.

The effect of the existing stock on the solution of any architectural problem is therefore likely to be considerable. It will be felt both by the users of buildings accustomed to the patterns of usage suggested by existing spaces and architects to whom these are inescapable models which they have to react in some way.

Very often this effect is masked because both user and designer come from a common culture and the assumptions which are the starting point are recognised in the same way by both. In real terms that common culture does not always exist. Class differences and the resulting different patterns of use of rooms in a house, for example, have been known to produce inappropriate plans for public housing because the designer was unaware of the explicit differences which existed. These class differences in both use and symbolic values were hidden because the architectural problem was set simply as the design of a 'house'.

The differences often become much more apparent when an architect works in a different country. When I was asked in 1980 to help in the design of the Institute of Scientific and Technical Information of China (ISTIC) on the edge of the centre of Beijing (Peking) my first reaction was to amend the proposal made by a group of Chinese architects which consisted of a four-storey podium and a thirteen-storey tower into a five-storey building with four

112 Michael Brawne
Institute of Scientific and Technical
Information of China, Bejing, 1980

courtyards. This solved many of the functional problems in the grouping of different parts of the library and made for simpler circulation and greater flexibility. It also reduced the amount of circulation space and thus improved the net to gross area ratio.

There was no doubt that I was influenced by the prevailing Western reaction against tall buildings, whereas my Chinese colleagues were very deeply imbued with notions of modern architecture derived from Soviet models. They agreed after a period of discussion that my suggestions were probably more functionally appropriate to the needs of ISTIC but that the resultant low form was not suitable for a 'national monument'; that the building would not be noticed. My counter-argument that the Imperial Palace in the centre of Beijing was even lower but could not fail to be acknowledged was not accepted. The group responsible for the planning of the city was then brought in and was equally doubtful about the correctness of a five-storey solution, despite my descriptions of how many Western cities regretted the intrusion of tall buildings close to their historic centres and how important it was to prevent a similar intrusion into an area visible from the Imperial Palace and its adjacent gardens.

131

In a sense I was asserting a colonial view in which the stranger presumes to know best and tries to instruct the 'native'. My current Western view was in conflict with a Chinese standpoint derived from a different and earlier Western model. Very similar discussions arose on the design of the enclosing wall. I designed an external skeleton structure which would support sun shading to reduce the impact of the very hot summers, and argued that such an outside framework with a strong horizontal emphasis was deeply rooted in traditional Chinese architecture. I was trying to work within some regional model. This was described by the Chinese architects as 'too novel' and therefore too difficult for them to assimilate. Current practice in Beijing produced smooth buildings in pre-cast concrete.

Some months after my departure I learned through Unesco that the general plan form and height were eventually agreed but it was unlikely that the exterior would be built as I had suggested. The other significant change was that the staff entrance, which I had placed on the north side adjacent to the staff living quarters and cafeteria, had been moved to the east because of 'the demands of access for fire fighting'. However, roads existed on both the north and east sides. I had been told in Beijing about the need to exclude the cold north wind from entrances and had therefore designed a glass-enclosed projecting vestibule with doors on the east and west sides. Very much later I learned that the old-established precepts of geomancy which governed the siting of houses and their entrances in China ruled out entrances on the north side. The user but not the designer was aware of an implicit code.

The existing stock is of course in a continual state of change. In the sense in which every building is in some measure a forecast of future patterns of use, the act of creating a building in a particular way itself affects that future. This is what Popper in the context of the social sciences has called the 'Oedipus effect', that is to say 'the influence of the prediction upon the predicted event . . whether this influence tends to bring about the predicted event, or whether it tends to prevent it'. Had there not been a prophecy about Oedipus's future impact on his parents, he would have grown up at home like any other Greek child, and it is extremely unlikely that he would subsequently have mistaken his father for a stranger at the crossroads, with fatal results, or married his mother. In very much the same way, by designing buildings in a way which makes certain actions or attitudes more probable, more easy to achieve, we influence the future which is able to react favourably or unfavourably to these possibilities; it may in many instances, of course, ignore them. The eventual establishment of Le Corbusier's prophetic vision of 'La Ville Radieuse', for instance, was made much less likely by the actual construction of some tall buildings in parkland, and the resulting public reaction.

The *second* crucial aspect of any architectural problem involves making decisions. It has two sub-groups: one which deals primarily with those decisions made by the client in the formulation of a set of requirements which is seen as a brief or a set of instructions, the other with those decisions made by the architect in the process of design. Decisions made by clients or client equivalents can be structured on some hierarchical basis, though they may not be made on any such set of ordered assumptions. The first decision must be whether the problem to be solved – the need to be met – can have an architectural solution: whether a new factory rather than new and more efficient machinery will improve production; whether new housing rather than in-creased occupancy of existing housing will deal with the homeless; whether education needs schools rather than using houses, offices, museums or factories to carry out its tasks; whether publicly available information should be stored in library buildings rather than being brought to the door in mobile vans or made accessible through computer consoles; or whether many aspects of work need to be performed in specially constructed workshops or offices, instead of at home. These are very basic decisions, often enormously influenced by our cultural bias, which define the architectural problem in its most general form in the sense that they establish that some kind of building is needed.

Once this primary decision has been made, some definition of the architectural task is as a rule attempted by those who are the effective commis-sioning agents for the building. The difficulty of translating such intentions into verbal and numerical instructions which will eventually correspond in an

133

unequivocal way with a building has already been discussed and is in any case not normally crucial to the kind of definition which is put forward at this stage. What most commonly happens is that a brief determines a site and lays down certain requirements by defining functions and space allocations, that it probably puts upper limits on expenditure, and that it may establish who is to carry responsibility for making decisions during the subsequent stages of the design and building process. Although such a brief does not determine a form, it provides guidelines and establishes certain goals which inevitably and properly restrict the choices open to the architect. But both the restriction of choice and the definition of requirements embedded in the brief are themselves largely derived from familiarity with a known situation, in other words from an awareness of existing buildings and their normal usage. These of necessity act as models for the hypothetical building implied by any set of instructions. To put it in an extreme form, it is enormously difficult to envisage how one would write a brief for a school or a hospital or even a house if such building types did not already exist. The definition of the problem is thus to a considerable extent dependent on previous history. And so, of course, is the solution. Significantly, Louis Kahn's definition of school as 'a man sitting under a tree talking to a student who didn't know he was a student, simply talking about what occurred to him as a realization' omits any mention of a building.

As often as not, a client will derive a brief by taking the design with which he is most familiar (probably the building he is currently occupying) and amending and enlarging it, as well as possibly drawing attention to its faults. The relationships between usage and space which are being specified are likely to involve only relatively small changes from what is known. The fact that, under more enlightened conditions, the architect and his consultants may be involved in the process of selecting a site and arriving at a brief does not fundamentally alter the situation; it is only likely to enlarge the range of models which come readily to mind. The initial decisions may thus be more widely influenced but are still dependent on the existence of available and usable models. Our decisions are therefore inevitably moulded by the category of the already given and known.

The acceptance of such models need not be uncritical; on the contrary, this is one of the crucial stages at which a critical examination of the assumptions behind the building ought to take place. The way in which university students are housed, for example, has been subjected to such criticism and as a result has undergone a considerable change during the building of the new universities in Britain from the middle 1960s onwards. Apart from living at home or in lodgings, students stayed traditionally either in college or in halls of residence. Colleges were largely confined to the older institutions and were particularly associated with Oxford and Cambridge and with St Andrew's in Scotland. At Oxford and Cambridge, the idea of the college had arisen from a functional association among a body of men who lodged together, some of them teachers and others students, and who had financial autonomy. Many of these characteristics survive to this day, despite the existence of the university as a teaching and administrative body. The college could be said still to have some functional reality. Halls of residence, on the other hand, had arisen at the universities which had grown up in a non-collegiate and often deliberately non-conformist way from the middle of the nineteenth century onwards, and which often had their origin in Technical Institutes or Medical Schools attended by students living at home. Halls were introduced when these universities became national institutions and attracted students from a wider region, because it was thought that some pseudo-collegiate grouping under a warden would provide the civilising and broadening influence associated with collegiate life. No functional reality, however, appeared to support this organisation, and to many students of the post-war period there seemed no basis to the rules which such halls imposed on their residents.

Both of these student living patterns were criticised by sociologists looking at arrangements for housing the growing number of students. The results of two surveys published in the *Universities Quarterly* in 1961 suggested that some alternative, less restrictive form would meet with wider approval; that students were mature adults who wanted more 'ordinary', more independent living arrangements.

Sociological research also seemed to show that

135

groups of between eight and twelve students were large enough to provide a sufficient variety of people to allow friendships to be formed but not so large as to appear an amorphous and unfamiliar set. From these considerations and from an awareness of some Scandinavian examples, briefs were formulated which asked for groupings of students about some common space within which they might also do some cooking: in college terms, a combination of an enlarged gyp-room with a miniature junior common room. Even before any built example of such a space was available, however, the term 'farmhouse kitchen' was often applied to it. There seemed to be a need to suggest a model, selected from the known range of available models, which could act as a guide. As a result of a criticism of existing provisions, the new brief for student residences thus suggested a model shift. The definition of the shift eventually depended on the fact that within the existing stock of buildings a prototype could be isolated. It also no doubt received some encouragement from literature, where the farm kitchen was seen as the centre of a richer family life that had existed in the past; this was the theme of descriptions such as those found in Mumford's biography of his son Geddes, where 'the kitchen was the great family domain . . . one of the best places for spontaneous family confidences', but perhaps most critically, 'the main thing about it was that it was spacious and many activities besides cooking went on there.'

Society, acting in a sense as the ultimate client, also performs a critical role. It does so politically by forms of financial control, as in the case of subsidies, and by using planning legislation to stop certain kinds of development or to insist on certain visual criteria or the use of particular materials. These tend to be negative controls. But it also plays a more subtle role. In recent years there has been a considerable shift from an enthusiasm for the new to a perhaps excessively tenacious belief in the virtues of the old. This has not only caused a great many old buildings to be preserved and refurbished but also affected the architect's search for a model. If in the 1930s the search was for a prototype among engineering structures such as grain silos or ships or motor cars, even though the eventual buildings were rarely affected by these models, today it is much more likely

113 House in Conogher, nr Dervock, Co. Antrim, Ulster, photographed c.1910

136

to be for some earlier building or urban setting. A housing development such as Robin Hood Gardens in the East End of London, designed by Alison and Peter Smithson for the Greater London Council in 1966, would have been described thirty year earlier and perhaps even ten years earlier in terms of social benefits and its physical novelty as a housing solution; the Smithsons' reference in 1972 when discussing the project is largely to Georgian squares.

The second sub-group includes all those decisions made by the architect and his consultants – structural and service engineers, quantity surveyors and cost advisers, contract management specialists – between the inception of the design process and the completion of the building. This set of decisions and the ideas behind them are of course the main preoccupation of this essay and have to some extent already been discussed. Most other issues – and there are a great many in any architectural task – have been looked at largely from the point of view of the effect they have on this particular process of making architectural decisions and thus, presumably, on the completed building. It is intended to continue this discussion in a subsequent section, with particular emphasis on the various steps of a design sequence.

Although existing technologies may limit choices or even totally exclude categories of the imaginable, and although the range of available models may reduce the number of possible starting points, nevertheless there is invariably a decision to be made about a preferred model and about options within any selected model. The agony and pleasure of selecting and deciding is inextricably locked into the process of design.

16

The *third* aspect, and clearly the most important, is the building which results from this complex set of considerations. It is the goal of the entire process and the reason for its inception; it demonstrates a commitment to certain specific decisions by a chain of institutions and individuals; it acquires an ability to influence new sets of decisions made by those who inhabit it and those who only look at it; it immediately becomes part of the existing stock, of the already given.

The complete building will be understood at a number of levels, but the way in which it is understood must always be primarily through the senses. Granted that architecture has an intellectual content, conveys social meanings or is able to alter some of our physiological and psychological states, nevertheless all of these attributes must initially be received through sensory perception. It is the visual, tactile and auditory effect of buildings which makes an impression on us and through which all other effects must be conveyed. This is especially true of the completed building as distinct from its earlier analysis, the drawing or a scale model. Clearly dominant among the senses involved must be the visual; an architecture which was not seen but only felt by our fingertips, sensed by our bodies through heat and cold or heard in the throwing back or muffling of sounds would in no way meet our expectations of the essential qualities of architecture. Its primary characteristic is inevitably visual.

The second dominant impression is not through one of the other four senses but through bodily movement – walking, reaching out, stooping – and the way these require physical effort; this is best described as the kinaesthetic sense, that 'sense of muscular effort that accompanies a voluntary motion of the body' (OED). Frequently this sensory experience is directly combined with the visual, and it could be argued that one of the most clearly distinguishable attributes of architecture is the way in which a moving observer senses visual images in sequence. The Ecole des Beaux Arts defined this as the *promenade architecturelle*: the way in which we sense a street, or take in the alternating rhythm of columns at

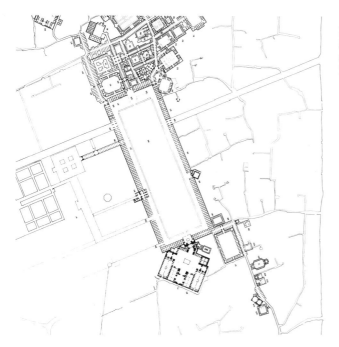

114 Plan of Maidan, Isfahan
Mosque of Sheikh Lutf Allah on east
side of Maidan; Mosque of the Shah,
1628–29, on south side of Maidan

Ely Cathedral as we move from the west door to the altar, are made to turn and experience different lighting conditions between the vast Maidan outside and the quibla wall within, oriented towards Mecca, in the mosque of Sheikh Lutf Allah at Isfahan. At other times it may cause an almost involuntary movement which will alter our visual impression, as in the case of the exceptionally low ceilings which characterise so many of Frank Lloyd Wright's buildings. Equally, our bodily posture will affect what we see and thus how a building might be organised. The fact that in Japan and throughout most of the Islamic world people sit on the floor, for example, has had the most significant and easily discernible effect on architecture.

The kinaesthetic sensation may even be primary and the visual secondary. It has much to do with the way we experience a single-storey house or flat as against a two-storey building; the way we sense the long staircase of the Trinità dei Monti (the Spanish Steps) in Rome by Francesco de Sanctis or the easy, gradual ascent of the grand staircase at the Opéra in Paris or the continuous inconvenience of a set of steps between kitchen and dining room, however visually satisfactory they might be.

115 Charles Garnier
Opéra, Paris, 1862–75, model grand
staircase

Perhaps precisely because moving up and down a staircase so effectively combines the visual and kinaesthetic experience of architecture, the design of the staircase was often a preoccupation, even an obsession, in periods of architecture when spatial complexity and its experience played an explicit role; the staircase is a dominant element of very many baroque and rococo designs.

It is also through the combined effects of vision, movement and memory that we experience the most abstract attributes of architecture. This integrated experience allows us to understand the plan and the spatial organisation of a building. The geometry of space, of whatever kind it may be, is sensed by seeing, moving and remembering what was seen and what the movement had been. As organisation is often closely related to the way in which we use the building, our feeling about appropriateness will also be the result of perceptions which we initially had visually and kinaesthetically.

116 Bom Jesus, near Braga, Portugal
steps to the pilgrimage church begun 1727, church c.1780

The architect's deepest concerns about purpose, order, appropriateness and proportion are involved in this continued experience. If 'architectural' could be applied as an adjective to a sensory experience, it would have to be used in precisely such a context, the highly complex and difficult to analyse experience of seeing, moving and remembering through which we understand and use space. The fact that we sense architecture in this way does not, however, say anything about its content or its meaning. The experience is only the means by which its attributes make their impact on us.

It seems that many of our feelings about space and particularly about its size are the result of a learning process which affects our reactions; a space in which we know that we can touch two walls at the same time with our arms outstretched feels different to one in which this is not possible. The same applies to ceilings which are or are not within reach. These reactions are modified and influenced by circumstances and by our expectations. Space standards for a corridor which we accept as normal in a railway carriage we would instantly dismiss as impossible in a house, although the number of people using it and wanting to pass is likely to be a good deal smaller. In both instances we are dealing with seeing and bodily movement and the sense of touch which is often closely related to it.

Many of our typical reactions to space, and therefore to architecture, are thus involved with a form of perception in which our visual and kinaesthetic senses are closely related. This is not to imply that sensory perception is the only element which affects the design process or which determines the final outcome. A programme of government subsidy for housing which allocates a specific amount of money for each dwelling will have a very direct effect on the kind of home which will eventually be used, and the effect will obviously be radically different if the amount of money is doubled. Our reactions to that home and our sensory perception of it will be considerably affected by its actual size (and therefore by the amount of money spent on it) and by our expectations of what constitutes an appropriate size in a particular set of circumstances. Such considerations, however, take us back to the first two categories, to the given elements and to the process of decision-making, especially the decisions made by those paying for the building.

An emphasis on the visual and the kinaesthetic is not intended to reduce the importance of what are often and perhaps mistakenly labelled the functional aspects of a building – the relationship between rooms, the efficacy of the plumbing, the watertightness of the roof or the convenience of the storage spaces. Undoubtedly, much of our satisfaction or dissatisfaction with buildings stems from the effect such aspects have on our daily usage; a great many of the complaints that are continually made by users about the work of architects have to do with precisely such problems. Yet it is clear that our reactions to buildings which we are not going to use, such as those made by a tourist on holiday, vary considerably and are therefore affected by feelings that have nothing to do with how such buildings might impinge on our comfort or our notions of convenience. And when actually buying a house, which will in the most direct way affect their pattern of life, different people will choose different houses within a particular price range not only on the basis of convenience or watertightness or heating efficiency, but on much more difficult to define grounds. I would argue that these have largely to do with the visual qualities of the house and its immediate surroundings. The complete range of functions of any building, considering the building as having both private and public impact, must include its function as a visually and kinaesthetically perceived object. This has been true about architecture throughout its history.

I would also argue that such an emphasis is in line with any reasonable definition of the aims of architecture. I take these to be the thoughtful construction or making of a defined place (space, enclosure . . .) for human use, whatever this may be – whether simply keeping warm or enshrining the symbols of a deity – with the proviso that that use must involve a direct experience of the constructed place. In terms of such a definition, an underground sewage tunnel is not an architectural problem, a pedestrian underpass is.

I believe such a distinction to correspond with practice. It is precisely because of the need to have this immediate and direct involvement that emphasis

142

on the visual and kinaesthetic experience is relevant, for it forms an essential part of that involvement.

Statements such as 'architecture must be functional' or 'architecture must satisfy human needs' or 'architecture is for people' are tautological. Of course these are true, it could not be otherwise. It is more interesting and more important to ask: 'what are the functions of architecture?' or 'what are people's needs?' Most important of all: 'how are we to deal with these questions?' and 'what answers are we to provide?' It could be said that any statement insisting that architecture is sensed most strongly by seeing and moving is also tautological, and I would not dissent from that view. What I am simply anxious to emphasise is that the *means* which architects have at their disposal to interpret and resolve the problems that they are set, or they set themselves, must make their first impression on any observer or user primarily through the visual and kinaesthetic senses.

17

These visual and kinaesthetic impressions are produced by the building; by its space, its light control,
its proportions, colours, textures and all the other
components which make up built form and which
invariably act together. This interlocking action of the
building elements has all the classic attributes of
Gestalt – of being more than the mere sum of the parts
– and is greatly dependent on scale, on the relation
between the dimensions of the building and those of
our bodies. This is the case not only because some
optical effects such as those of colour are influenced
by size but particularly because our bodily reactions
are so intimately related to the actual dimensions of
the space in which we move. It needs, therefore, a
built reality to create architectural impressions;
drawings or models or verbal descriptions can only
give a very partial experience, which itself is largely
dependent on our memory of the effects provided by
situations which we recall as being in some way
analogous to those represented on the drawing or in
the model. Architecture, as a set of ideas or concepts,
could be said to *exist* the moment it is drawn;
nevertheless it requires for its proper *understanding* to
be translated into building.

In this sense, a building could be considered as a
means of communication between the architect and
the user. It embodies the messages which formed
part of its design and which are eventually received
by those who see and use the building. There is,
however, no assurance of an inevitable correspondence between the initial messages and the subsequent reception. Many aspects of any communication
will always remain ambiguous – both intentionally
and unintentionally – and our reactions will change
over time, quite apart from being culturally influenced. In these respects architecture is closely akin to
other means of communication which act as the
bridge between two mental constructs.

To suggest because of this likeness that architecture
is also like language, and to try and understand
architecture through this analogy, appears to me to
raise more difficulties than it is likely to solve. The
comparison may in any case be trivial since it does no
more than draw attention to those attributes which

are common to all means of communication. The dangers, I believe, lie in suggesting that there are rules which have to be observed, as in grammar, in order for there to be any kind of comprehension, and that these rules have some innate structure which corresponds to our mental make-up or which are intuitively transmitted from generation to generation. Moreover, language is a much more basic and universal human attribute than the making of buildings; there are many people in any society who may never be involved in the creation of spaces throughout their lifetime. Language is also a much more abstract method of communication than architecture; words making a sentence must convey a meaning that relates wholly to something that exists outside that sentence. Only onomatopoeia in any way suggests meaning within the word. A building may indeed convey meanings that exist outside that particular set of spaces, but it will also carry messages that are inherent in the building elements themselves. A Doric order may carry symbolic connotations of masculinity (as distinct from Ionic, which Vitruvius described in Book IV as being 'characteristic of the slenderness of women', and Corinthian, 'an imitation of the slenderness of a maiden'), to take an example from the classical orders, but it also always conveys the impression of acting as a support, whether or not it actually does so. In other words it is extremely difficult, perhaps even impossible, to conceive that all the meanings of architecture could always be externalised.

The fact that any strongly pursued analogy between architecture and language may have serious pitfalls does not invalidate the notion of architecture as a means of communication. On the contrary, it emphasises the autonomy of architectural communication and suggests that the messages it may convey are peculiarly its own and different from those of verbal language.

Many of the decisions which are inescapably part of the design process must therefore concern themselves with the nature of the messages to be conveyed by the building. Much of design is thus directly involved in architectural communication, and in so far as design also involves criticism it will largely concern itself with a criticism of the messages being communicated – or, perhaps more precisely, with

145

messages previously communicated and now seen to be in some way unsatisfactory. The evidence for such criticism will be found in the difference which can be discerned between any two sets of messages.

I am not suggesting that all the differences which occur between one building and another, even if their functions are very similar, are entirely due to the fact that the later building can be seen as a criticism of the earlier one. This would be to ignore entirely the effect of chance as well as of personal design habits, both of which are often difficult to trace but which anyone involved in the process of making decisions while designing would recognise as being important. It would also ignore general changes in the options which are open when designing. What I am suggesting is that certain significant differences, which we recognise as a rule quite readily and see to be conveying some meaning, stem from such criticism; in particular, most model shifts are caused by just such criticism having taken place at a more profound and rigorous level. I am encouraged in this view by the difference between vernacular and non-vernacular architecture which is generally sensed without requiring specialist knowledge and which can be made without in any way implying a greater liking for one rather than the other.

When Nikolaus Pevsner opened *An Outline of European Architecture* with the sentence 'A bicycle shed is a building; Lincoln Cathedral is a piece of architecture' (which has already been quoted) he is

117 *Kersey, Suffolk*

presumably trying to define and thus limit the range of subject matter he proposes to discuss. He bases this distinction on the belief that 'the term architecture applies only to buildings designed with a view to aesthetic appeal'. Unless the term 'aesthetic' is to have an extremely narrow and uncommon meaning, that distinction would be very hard to apply. A moment's scanning of visual memories of sheds – whether for bicycles or cows or garden implements – would soon bring up examples which appealed visually even after all possible sentimental overtones had been subdued. Yet we would still continue to recognise the inherent difference in terms of architecture between a shed and a cathedral.

The distinction is, I believe, due to the nature and number of messages which each of these buildings is conveying; to the difference in their information content, both actual and intended.

A group of houses in a Suffolk village or on the alleyways of San'a in North Yemen differ one from the other only very slightly; the established model is persuasive and generally left uncriticised. The

118 San'a, Yemen

147

changes that occur are more often due to chance and very personal notions rather than to criticism of the existing stock. Where such criticism occurs it does so very gradually and usually only affects small elements of the building at a time. Although vernacular buildings clearly carry a great deal of meaning, much of it is in these small and separate elements of building rather than in their totality. The considerable historical continuity of the vernacular can thus be ascribed to the existence of a feeling that there is no need for rigorous criticism and that there is sufficient latitude for the degree of personal expression felt to be necessary or desirable. Indeed, perhaps this feeling exists because the content of vernacular architecture in terms of meaning is seen to be limited.

Non-vernacular architecture can probably be distinguished from its vernacular counterpart at any period by having a higher meaning content – intended or achieved – which can be discerned both in the building elements and in the building as a whole. The difference between Lincoln Cathedral and a bicycle shed is thus, I suggest, not the difference in aesthetic appeal – again intended or achieved – but in the content of the architectural messages each is communicating. Lincoln Cathedral can be described as architecture because of the nature and density of its communication.

To put it in a way which may risk a dangerous analogy, Lincoln Cathedral is an explanation of an architectural hypothesis with much greater content than that of a vernacular building; the hypothesis having arisen from a situation in which a number of architectural problems can be seen to require solution, can be criticised and an explanation eventually synthesised – an explanation which cannot, however, be trivial. The analogy is with theories in the natural sciences which are explanations of phenomena and particularly of relationships. It can be argued, as Karl Popper has done on a number of occasions, that the likelihood of a theory being falsified increases as its content increases; the more it explains the more probable it is that it will be proved wrong. To state an obvious and trivial truth is to risk nothing.

'"All tables are tables" is certainly true – it is more certainly true than Newton's and Einstein's theories of gravitation – but it is intellectually unexciting: it is

148

not what we are after in Science. Wilhelm Busch once produced what I have called a rhyme for the epistemological nursery:

Twice two equals four: 'tis true
But too empty and too trite
What I look for is a clue
To some matters not so light.

In other words, we are not simply looking for truth, we are after interesting and enlightening truth, after theories which offer solutions to interesting *problems*. If at all possible we are after deep theories.'

On this analogy, non-vernacular buildings could be described as those which offer solutions to the more interesting problems and even offer deep explanations to architectural questions. But in doing so, of course, they take greater risks and may be more easily criticised. This may to some extent explain the lesser historical stability of non-vernacular architecture as well as the fact that radical model shifts, especially those which we immediately recognise as the stylistic changes which gave labels to periods of history, occur in non-vernacular building.

We also recognise intuitively that such architectural explanations at any level of content are not general but particular, that in the case of vernacular architecture they are particular to a place and in the case of non-vernacular architecture to both place and time. For most people it is hard to date accurately the buildings on the Suffolk lane or the Yemen hillside, both historically and in relation to each other. It is, what is more, a question in which we are not greatly interested as a rule. The same cannot be said of non-vernacular building. What disturbs us at the sight of von Klenze's Walhalla above the Danube is not only that we see forms which we know to have their origin in Greece – such borrowing after all occurs in every neo-classical building – but that we are apparently confronted with an exact replica of a building which we know was designed over two thousand years earlier; we somehow cannot believe that the same explanation can still hold.

The point which has been made about the nature of theories and their content in relation to possible falsehood, and which by analogy I have extended to buildings, can in a sense be made about most statements. I am entirely aware that by making this analogy, for example, I increase the risk of some of the notions put forward in this section, or perhaps in the whole essay, being refuted and, what is probably more crucial, being refuted more readily. I make the analogy, however, not only because I believe in its validity, but largely because I am interested in its usefulness, in its fertility. I hold for instance, that it helps us to understand something about the differences between categories of buildings, levels of expressiveness, differences in the rate of stylistic change, the function of critical attitudes in design and thus, by extension, the needs of architectural education and historical criticism.

18

The necessity for criticism, even if accepted, says nothing about the reasons for such criticism or what may influence its severity. We know that change occurs; I am suggesting that a great deal of change is the result of criticism and the rejection of established models or at least their deliberate modification. We are extremely uncertain, though, about the causes of such criticism, about the initial dissatisfaction which in some way refuses to repeat in its entirety the already known and established, particularly in non-vernacular architecture.

If a building can in some sense be considered as a means of communication, it can also be argued that at certain times its messages may cease to be appropriate; we may no longer feel that there is a match between the explanation being made and the problem as we understand it. This may occur because the problem has in fact altered or because, through repetition, it has simply become banal. But in non-vernacular architecture we expect explanations of complex situations and are, as a rule, unwilling to accept banal answers for long. There are other times when the extreme novelty of an answer may go so far beyond expectation that it is rejected. This is often particularly the case in housing, which for centuries has largely been part of vernacular architecture and where novelty is therefore not greatly prized. Problem, expectation and answer have all evidently to be related.

The following protest letter, signed by a considerable number of artists, appeared in *Le temps* on 14 February 1887:

'Writers, painters, sculptors, architects, passionate lovers of beauty, until now unspoilt, of Paris, we come to protest with all our strength, with all our indignation, in the name of disregarded French taste, in the name of art and French history presently in danger, against the erection, in the very heart of our capital, of the useless and monstrous Eiffel Tower . . . Will this city of Paris continue to listen to the baroque, mercantile fancies of a builder of machines, and irreparably lose its honour and beauty? For the Eiffel Tower, which even the

119 *Eiffel Tower, Paris, 1889*
a view of the tower made up of 300
lines of verse

commercial America would reject, means, without any doubt, a Paris dishonoured. Everyone feels this, everyone says it, everyone is deeply hurt and we are only a weak echo of this universal opinion, so legitimately alarmed. Indeed, when the people of other countries finally come to visit our Exposition, they will cry in astonishment: "What? – is this horror that the French have brought forth to give us an idea of their famous taste?" They will be right in mocking us, for the Paris of sublime Gothic Art, the Paris of Jean Goujon, of Germain Pilon, of Puget, of Rude, of Barye etc. will have become the Paris of Monsieur Eiffel.' (The signatures included E. Meissonier, Charles Gounod, Charles Garnier, W. Bougneveau, A. Dumas, François Coppée, Leconte de Lisle, Sully Prudhomme and Guy de Maupassant.)

And of course they were right: the Eiffel Tower has become the symbol of Paris. Its instant recognition on posters, in films, or on a postcard immediately arouses an association with Paris. The important point for this argument, however, is not the rightness or wrongness of that particular group of Parisian artists, or even the tone of their letter and the strange association of the Eiffel Tower, which must surely rank among the world's less useful constructions, with American commercialism, but the fact that it was constructed for the Paris Exposition of 1889. The rejection of the protest by such a highly influential group was due not only to the shrewdness of the chairman of the exhibition committee, Jean Alphaud, who was both an engineer and a landscape architect and who had created a series of great parks in Paris under Haussmann, but also, one suspects, to the fact that our expectations of what is appropriate and acceptable are considerably altered at the time of a special event such as a great exhibition. The unusual becomes almost the norm.

The Paris Exposition of 1889 was by no means unique in this respect. One of the most remarkable buildings of the nineteenth century had been created for the Great Exhibition of 1851 in London by Joseph Paxton, after the Commission had rejected 245 plans submitted to it. The Crystal Palace, 1851 ft (564 m) long, 124 m wide, and in places 33 m high, had the first column erected on 26 September 1850. Its main work was complete by 12 February 1851 (20 weeks

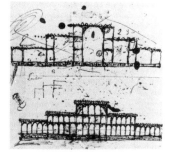

120 J Paxton
Crystal Palace, London, blotting paper sketch made on 7 June 1850 during a board meeting of the Midland Railway of which Paxton was a director

152

later) and it was opened on time by Queen Victoria on 1 May 1851. Having been created under these unusual circumstances, it modified nineteenth-century expectations, especially so far as a great many subsequent exhibitions were concerned.

In a very similar way, two important exhibitions held in Paris in this century were able to introduce or diffuse an innovatory style: that of 1900, Art Nouveau, and that of 1925, what later became known as Art Deco after the exhibition's ponderous title of Exposition Internationale des Arts Decoratifs et Industriels Modernes. The view of what would be appropriate was also conditioned by the relation of one exhibition to another: 'The previous Exposition in Paris, of 1900, was universally remembered as the peak moment of French Art Nouveau, and had been succeeded by a tidal wave of imitation so strong that it was soon swept rather out of fashion – its ever-present muse a full-bosomed, heavy-hipped *femme fatale*, of long streaming hair, self-absorbed, languishing, voluptuous; its constant motifs drawing on a naturalistic study of sinuous tendrils and the frailer flowers. The organisers now of 1925 were determined to distil a truly modern style, fit for the next generation, that would differ in almost every conceivable way from the spirit of the last.'

Although a particular event may cause a problem to be restated in a new way and may at the same time make a radical answer feasible, the nature of the answer can take many forms and can stem from different critical points of view – technological in Paris in 1889, stylistic in 1925 – even though the underlying search for novelty may be the same at both times. It seems important therefore to distinguish between the dissatisfaction which we may feel with the currently produced answer, the accepted explanation, and that part of the answer which we select for critical amendment. Arguably, these two aspects should be closely related, yet I believe that this is by no means a foregone conclusion.

When we look at the west side of Le Corbusier's Chapel at Ronchamp, we immediately sense the play of tone, texture and light between the white wall and the grey shuttered concrete of the gargoyle and of the water basin. The concrete surface is marked by each timber board of the shuttering, which has left the imprint of its rough wood grain. It is a technique

121 Crystal Palace, scene on 1 May 1851 as Queen Victoria declared the Great Exhibition open

153

122 *Le Corbusier*
Notre-Dame du Haut, Ronchamp,
1950–55

which had already come into evidence at the earlier Unité d'Habitation in Marseilles and which was very different from the smooth white surfaces which had been characteristic of Le Corbusier's pre-war buildings, though not exclusively so. The question which the gargoyle and the sculptural water basin therefore pose are whether the *béton brut* is the result of immediate post-war shortages of money and materials; of a desire to create a decorated surface without recourse to the accepted means of wall decoration; of a moral stance to use materials in their natural state; of a need to reintroduce organic-looking surfaces and forms into architecture, which had seemingly become too technological; or of an attempt to create some symbolic interplay between water and earth. All or none of these hypothetical questions could be relevant. I believe that in any situation of this kind a number of criticisms are invariably at work, modified as a rule by the state of those elements which could be considered as being given, and that it is this combination of critical attitudes which alters the answer. It is not a case of simple cause and effect. Moreover, I take this emphasis on a multiplicity of criticisms related to different aspects of architecture to be in line with the earlier argument that architectural solutions cannot be specified in their entirety by statements that can exist outside architecture, say by verbal or numerical means. If this were not so, it could perhaps be suggested that if the criticisms could be defined and isolated and could also be shown to be the only and necessary causes of architectural solutions then through the definition of criticisms we could indeed define architectural answers. I do not, however, believe that such a suggestion can be validated.

To state it in another way, I would hold that there is no invariably direct relation between the cause of our unwillingness to accept an answer, which then stimulates the initial criticism, and those parts of the building which are actually subjected to critical change. Recent architectural history, for instance, is littered with instances of verbal critical statements, of a social and political nature, which suggest dramatic planning and organisational differences but actually cause only minor elevational changes. There is no certainty in architecture that criticism of one element will produce a significant alteration to that particular

154

element, or that if we observe a shift in some aspect it will inevitably have resulted from an earlier criticism of that aspect. It will usually have done so, but it would be unwise and unsafe to make claims of an inevitable lock between cause and effect.

This difficulty applies both to the kind of design criticism being discussed here and to the historical criticism of building and movements undertaken long after the design decisions have been taken. It is, one suspects, just this kind of uncertainty which prompts Alan Colquhoun to begin his essay on Michael Graves, one of the New York Five, with the following words: 'Criticism occupies the no-man's land between enthusiasm and doubt, between poetic sympathy and analysis. Its purpose is not, except in unique cases, either to eulogize or to condemn' – and then he adds the important qualification 'and it can never grasp the essence of the work it discusses'.

The fact that it may not always be possible to isolate and define all the criticisms which initiate the translation from one tentative solution to another does not mean that such criticism does not take place. It only suggests that instead of looking for precise causes or definitions it may be more useful and interesting to look at processes, to look in particular at the process which takes place between the initial design idea and the completed inhabited building and to assess the role of criticism and the role of models in that sequence.

The *first* example is a documented sequence of preliminary designs by one of the most important American architects of the middle of this century, Louis Kahn, for a building designed only a few years before his death. References to earlier work are immediately noticeable.

To use one's earlier work as a model is natural since it is not only part of the general existing stock but, more to the point, presumably very much part of the individual's mental stock. It is this use of a limited range of models and their modification which gives the work of an artist or designer its characteristic handwriting; it is through the repetition of traits that we recognise a Matisse painting or an Aalto building. As this is such a natural tendency it may occasionally lead to the initial selection of an inappropriate model, which may only be rectified later through criticism in the design process or may even survive with

123 *Louis I Kahn*
Kimbell Art Museum, Fort Worth,
Texas, 1969–1972
aerial view

unsatisfactory implications in the completed building.

In 1967 Louis Kahn was asked to design a small museum in Fort Worth, Texas, to house the collection of European and Asian paintings and sculpture which the Kimbell family had acquired. The museum is a two-storey reinforced concrete structure with the upper floor at the same level as the park, and consisting of 16 vaulted units 6.5 metres wide by 30 metres long. As in the case of so many of Kahn's buildings, there is an assembly of individually constructed units each clearly articulated. The galleries are under ten of these cycloidal vaults making partly defined spaces, almost domestic in character, like the Catalan vaulted spaces of Le Corbusier's Maison Jaoul or the Sarabhai house in Ahmedabad, but somehow also Byzantine in feeling.

What distinguishes these particular vaults is that they have a continuous slit in their crown, letting in a small amount of daylight which is diffused and reflected by a perforated aluminium shield underneath it. Light is thus thrown back on to the vault, which becomes bright, and at the same time is filtered down into the centre of the gallery.

In 1969 Kahn was appointed as architect of what was eventually to be called the Yale Center for British Art in New Haven, Connecticut. Paul Mellon had in 1966 given to his old university the collection of British art which he had put together and which was

124 *Louis I Kahn*
Kimbell Art Museum, Fort Worth,
Texas, 1969–1972
south entrance

156

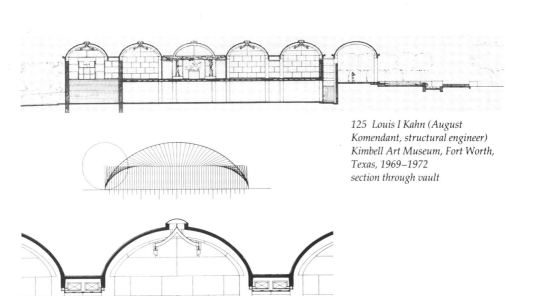

125 Louis I Kahn (August
Komendant, structural engineer)
Kimbell Art Museum, Fort Worth,
Texas, 1969–1972
section through vault

126 Louis I Kahn
Kimbell Art Museum, Fort Worth,
Texas, 1969–1972
view of two adjacent galleries

considered unrivalled outside England. He also provided funds for land, a building and the endowment of the centre. Kahn was chosen because, as the director of the centre wrote in 1969:

'Louis Kahn is, in my opinion, the greatest American architect of our time, uniquely equipped to respond to the opportunity afforded Yale and New Haven by Paul Mellon's gift. He is a remarkable human being, sensitive both to the inner world of art and the external world of everyday experience . . . Kahn's previous accomplishments suggest that he will create a building that will be strong and positive, but not monumental. He is a friend of daylight, and a master at introducing it wherever the program requires.'

The site for the building was on the same street and virtually opposite the Yale University Art Gallery which Kahn had designed in 1951 and where in the Art and Architectural Building he had taught for many years.

The final preliminary design was presented in March 1971. It was a four-storey building in which

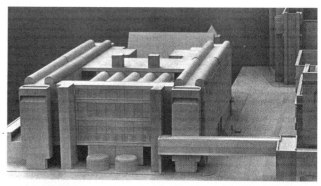

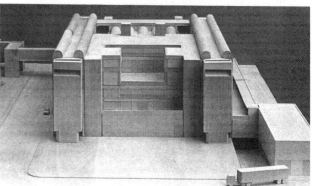

127 *Louis I Kahn*
Yale Center for British Art, New Haven, Conn.
Model, March 1971

158

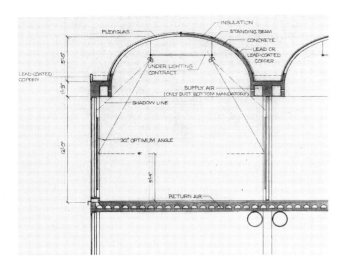

128 Louis I Kahn
Yale Center for British Art, New Haven, Conn.
section of bay with skylight, September 1971

the main gallery spaces were on the top floor so that they could receive daylight through the roof. Although the details of controlling what was then assumed to be north light had not been worked out, both in plan form and section there was a considerable resemblance to the Kimbell Art Museum. Kahn had, as it were, lifted the long vaulted galleries and placed them as the crowning floor of his multi-storey complex in New Haven.

At the centre of the plan there was also a great covered courtyard, just as a three-sided court formed the focus of the galleries at Fort Worth. But at Yale it was to be a multi-storey court, like that of a palazzo, and again in plan and section very like the central space of Kahn's Phillips Exeter Academy Library in New Hampshire of 1967–72.

In other words, two of Kahn's most recent designs for buildings which in their programme were akin to the Center for British Art became models and were combined to form a new design. Other features, such as the use of great trusses which he had proposed for the Palazzo de Congressi in Venice in 1969, were also in evidence. His 'handwriting' was unmistakable.

When cost estimates were made it was found that the spring 1971 proposals exceeded the available budget owing to rapid inflation in building prices. The programme had to be reduced by about a third of the floor area.

The second design, presented in the autumn of 1971, differs in a number of important points from the

129 Louis I Kahn
Yale Center for British Art, New Haven, Conn.
sketch of entrance court with skylights, 1971

130 Louis I Kahn
Library, Phillips Academy, New Hampshire, 1967–72
central hall

first. The entrance has been moved to the corner; there are now two smaller covered courts; the exterior is simpler, less shaped; the large vierendeel trusses have been abandoned as cars are no longer parked in the basement. The most important alteration, however, is in the top floor. The main area of exhibition is now a 'family' of 6 m (20 ft) square spaces defined by corner columns and each with a square rooflight which was eventually to be developed by Richard Kelly, the lighting consultant, and by Pellechia and Myers, the architects who completed the building after Kahn's untimely death in March 1974. What is of immediate interest is that these square rooms have many of the attributes of the Trenton Bath House of 1954–59, one of Kahn's earliest projects to receive international recognition despite its extremely modest size and simplicity.

Kahn thus returns to his most deep-rooted geometrical preoccupation, the square with its bi-axial symmetry, and the making of spaces through the juxtaposition of such squares. In addition, this use of square room-like forms clustered about open halls is close to the plan forms of an English country

131 Louis I Kahn
Yale Center for British Art, New Haven, Conn. 1973–77
plan of top floor

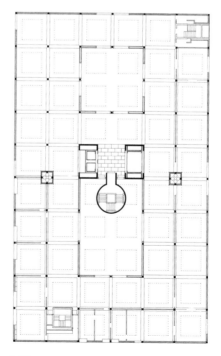

160

house – the original home of much of the art on display – which Kahn had wanted to evoke. Two groups of models could thus be said to be in evidence: those arising from Kahn's own earlier designs and those suggesting themselves from the nature of the programme. The first appears much more dominant than the second.

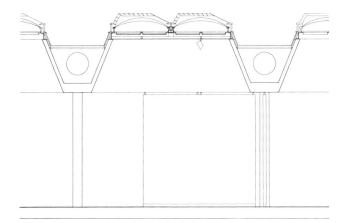

132 *Louis I Kahn*
Yale Center for British Art, New Haven, Conn. 1973–77
top floor, typical bay and section through skylight (Richard Kelly, lighting consultant)

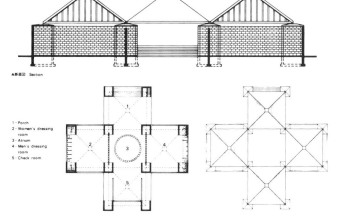

133 *Louis I Kahn*
Bath House, Trenton, New Jersey, 1954–59

19

It could be argued that Kahn had always worked with a limited set of forms, particularly a limited range of geometries usually characterised by bi-axial symmetry, and that it was therefore only to be expected that he should turn to an earlier museum of his at the start of the design of a subsequent one, however different the locality or programme. To put it another way, Kahn had always availed himself of only a limited group of models. His visual preferences are certainly well known both from his talks and from his travel sketchbooks. To counter this objection I intend to use as my *second* example the work of an architect in Sri Lanka whose formal vocabulary has undergone a marked change and whose ideas are familiar to me from frequent discussions.

During a conversation in 1982, sitting in his study at the far end of his house in Colombo, Geoffrey Bawa was outlining a proposal to send Sri Lankan students of architecture on a study tour of India. They would perhaps start at the marvellous palace complex of Padmanabhapuram in Kerala, sit under the red sandstone roof of an open pavilion at Fathepur Sikri, have tea at the Taj Mahal Hotel in Bombay, and eventually reach the carved stone city of Jaisalmer at the far end of the Sind plain. Bawa then added almost as an afterthought, but nevertheless as an important aspect of such a journey, ' . . . and they need not even see a single modern building'. It is, I suspect, not a comment he would have made in 1957 on his return from studying in England, or even more than a decade later when designing the Ceylon Pavilion for Expo '70 at Osaka.

The difference between these two positions is not only a measure of the change which has occurred in architectural thought in general in almost every country but also perhaps a clue to Geoffrey Bawa's own development and the contribution he has made to architecture in Sri Lanka and elsewhere – a contribution acknowledged by the award of the Gold Medal of the Sri Lanka Institute of Architects in November 1982.

Architectural education presupposes that something can be taught and that there is at least some process which can be handed down to others and

134 Padmanabhapuram Palace, Kerala, India, 15th–18th century

135 Fathepur Sikri, Agra, India, c.1570
Panch Mahal (terraces for the ladies of the zenana)

136 *House, Jaisalmer, west of Jodhpur, India*

which goes beyond the communication of purely factual knowledge. This supposition is clearly behind Geoffrey Bawa's belief that an architectural student would benefit from seeing and understanding certain Indian buildings; if it were entirely a matter of intuitive feeling there would be no need for any kind of learning.

The idea of travel suggests moreover a particular form of learning. It assumes, I believe, that an awareness of the work of others can be of benefit, particularly in this case, the work of one's predecessors within a very similar cultural context. Behind this assumption there is perhaps another and more fundamental notion: namely that a great deal of design starts from a familiarity with a range of architecture and that we choose from that range certain aspects which become the models for our

137 *Geoffrey Bawa
Ceylon Pavilion, Expo 1970, Osaka*

163

design. The choice of an appropriate model is always difficult but always crucial. Frequently it is easier to decide what not to do than to fix on what to select, hence the exclusion of contemporary buildings from the itinerary.

The development which can be seen in the work of Geoffrey Bawa can perhaps also be described as a gradual shift from European to Asian models. Asian architecture has long and varied traditions, which in a great number of countries and at different periods have produced a remarkable range of buildings that are important to the architectural heritage of the whole world. No discussion of architectural history in general could sensibly omit the Mughal buildings of the Indian subcontinent or the temples and palaces of Japan, for example. Yet in many Asian countries the indigenous traditions became weak or even non-existent in the last hundred years or so. Any awakening of these architectural roots is obviously of importance to the development of a regional architecture; one of Geoffrey Bawa's contributions has been a visible acknowledgement of such Asian, and particularly South Asian, traditions.

Architectural ideas, particularly our attitude towards the past, have altered considerably during the past twenty years. The work of Geoffrey Bawa has been part of that change; it has contributed to it and has in turn itself been made more possible by the currency of these ideas. Some of the tendencies towards a different kind of architecture were probably developed in association with Ulrik Plesner, who collaborated with Bawa for a number of years and who had previously worked with Minnette de Silva in Kandy. Plesner came to Sri Lanka from Denmark, where a traditional architectural vocabulary had for a long time been acceptable and had been greatly enriched in the late 1950s and early 1960s by architects such as Jørn Utzon, whose housing groups at Elsinore and at Fredensborg were immediately influential.

It would be wrong to assume, however, that the change and development which can be traced in the designs of Geoffrey Bawa are purely ones of style, of substituting pitched roofs for flat ones, or of decorating buildings with works of art. There has also, I would argue, been an important shift in the way buildings are planned and space is manipulated.

138 Jørn Utzon
Housing at Fredensborg, Denmark,
1963
club house

164

The really significant difference can best be seen if one compares two groups of buildings: the first would include the house for Wijeyawardena, the Chapel of the Good Shepherd at Bandarawela, perhaps even the doctor's house at Galle; the second, such houses as that for de Silva on Alfred Place, the house at Cambridge Place, the architect's own offices on Alfred House Road (originally designed as a house), the architect's own house off Bagatalle Road or the conversion of the house opposite. In the first group the building is a cubicular volume designed as an entity within a site; in the second there is a site which has been treated as a whole and within which

139 Geoffrey Bawa
Upali Wijeyawardene House,
Colombo, 1964

Section.

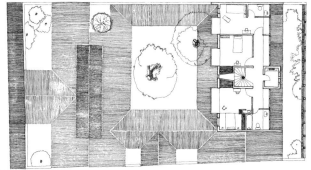

First floor plan.

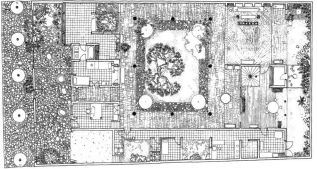

Ground floor plan.

140 Geoffrey Bawa
Ena de Silva House, Colombo, 1962
plan

165

141 *Geoffrey Bawa*
Ena de Silva House, Colombo, 1962
view through courtyards

there is a sequence of open and enclosed spaces. This sequence is, as a rule, a layering of space parallel to the street and one's movement through the building reveals alternately roofed and unroofed rooms. The first conception of space stems largely from the modern movement in architecture, where since the period of neo-classicism buildings have largely been thought of as pavilions, as isolated and individual creations. The second is a reworking of the concepts which governed the making of most Islamic or Chinese cities. It is a way of thinking of the town as

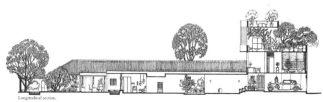

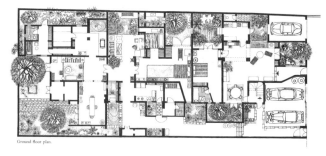

142 *Geoffrey Bawa*
Architect's own house, Colombo, 1957–68
plan and section

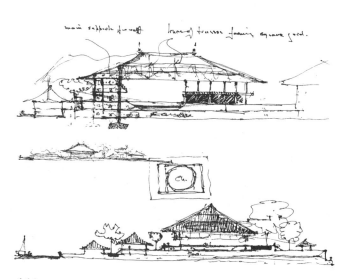

143 *Geoffrey Bawa*
New Parliamentary Complex, Sri Jayawardenepura, Kotte, Sri Lanka, 1982
preliminary sketches by the architect

166

consisting of public routes and of private spaces behind these, hollowed out as it were from a continuous layer of building. This pattern of making towns conformed not only to well-established cultural patterns but was extremely efficient in land use.

The new Parliament complex which was completed in 1982 was an enormous architectural opportunity and probably the most complex and demanding task ever tackled by Geoffrey Bawa and his office. Both in size and importance it dwarfs every previous project. There were no clear-cut precedents, particularly if one looks for examples outside Europe and America. Is Parliament a palace – as in the Palace of Westminster – or an office block with a large hall attached? That it is a national monument which is to be a symbol for a whole country and that it is also to be seen to be part of the life of that nation is not in doubt; what is much less clear is how to achieve that within an architectural tradition possessing few extant examples of very large buildings. Where there is an indication, as in the temple complexes, it suggests that large constructions were always groupings of lesser buildings. It is precisely this that has been done on the island within its new lake at Sri Jayawardenepura on the edge of Colombo.

The group is organised more or less symmetrically about an axis, a form of ordering which hierarchically important buildings have followed for centuries in both Asian and Western cultures. Each element of the group has a dominant roof clad in copper strips, the roof being a deep-rooted symbol of shelter and, in all tropical countries, at the same time the most vital part of any enclosure. The exterior, large parts of which

144 Geoffrey Bawa
New Parliamentary Complex, Sri Jayawardenepura, Kotte, Sri Lanka, 1982
view of buildings on the island

are beautifully constructed in hardwood, is a series of grilles and terraces which shield an inner line of glazing. All these aspects seem wholly in tune with a building in Sri Lanka.

What appears less so is the planning of the interior. This has adopted the close-knit pattern of corridors with rooms on either side which we associate with the making of a tight enclosure which has to be mechanically air-conditioned; it is a pattern prevalent in Europe and North America. What one misses is that cunning scooping out of space which produces courtyards and dappled light deep in what would otherwise be the interior of a building. It is difficult to relate oneself to the luxuriant outside as one walks down the corridors with their false ceilings and spots of artificial light. This artificial internal environment, I believe, creates in the last resort an architecture which does not echo the traditions of Sri Lanka. What one also misses at times is some continuity of space which orders the building as a whole and which orients movement through it. The great central debating chamber, hung with silver banners, cannot, because of its function, fulfil that role.

While it is true to say that we should only be interested in the building as a final product because this is what society uses, it would be equally wrong to pretend that, particularly as architects, we are not interested in the process by which it was made. Parliament was designed in an exceptionally short time and built by a foreign contractor who required information and decisions well ahead of the actual

146 Geoffrey Bawa
University of Ruhunu, Matara, Sri
Lanka, 1984–88
Physics Building

168

time of building. A great many designs in Sri Lanka are not carried out that way. Changes are made on site, various forms are tried out and only then is a decision given. The sight of Geoffrey Bawa leaning against a shooting stick ordering workmen to make some mock-up on site is one which many European architects deeply envy; it is a luxury which their forms of contract do not allow.

This way of designing and building leads frequently to the creation of incidents and local variations of space which provide pleasure within some more generally established framework. It is precisely such incidents which have characterised Bawa's most successful work. It may well be that certain models, to be fully successful, need corresponding design and building processes. Certainly at the new University of Ruhunu in the south of the island, under construction from 1984 onwards, one can immediately sense the presence of those elements which seem to be missing in the Parliament complex. But then the university is an assemblage of buildings on a hillside built in sequence over a period of time and linked by covered ways and great terraces and stairs.

The suggestion that the tour of India should include tea at the Taj might at first seem like the sort of flippant remark, made partly to shock, which Geoffrey Bawa makes from time to time. I do not believe it was in this case. It stemmed, I would argue, from a deep-seated belief that architecture plays an important role in making our lives fuller and richer; that tea at the Taj will not be the same as tea elsewhere and that somehow the simple act of having tea will be celebrated by the surroundings in which it occurs. That this motivates the designs of the hotels which have done so much to establish Bawa's reputation is perhaps obvious. It is equally evident in the very simple and sparse buildings of the farm school at Hanwella or those of the Integral Education Centre at Piliyandala.

Just as the stepped terraces of the Panch Mahal at Fatehpur Sikri, the Emperor Akbar's new city outside Agra, make sitting in the evening breeze an architectural event which then enhances that act, so the wide-open entrances of the Triton Hotel, which merges with the swimming pool and the sea as apparently one single floor plane, celebrates entering a hotel on a tropical island. Architecture turns our

147 Geoffrey Bawa
Integral Education Centre,
Piliyandala, Sri Lanka, 1981
link corridor

169

148 *Geoffrey Bawa*
Triton Hotel, Ahungalla, Sri Lanka,
1981
view from lobby to the pool and the
sea

dreams into reality. It does so in this instance because it rejects the European stereotype hotel and capitalises on the specific possibilities of the locality.

In the same way, moving through a stone tunnel and up a staircase under a batik ceiling to emerge at the side of a courtyard filled with a pool and to see beyond it the breakers on the shore makes the entrance into the Bentota Beach Hotel an experience which remains in the mind. With equal ingenuity the stairs, ramps and bridges at the Triton Hotel make pleasurable the journey from the dining room or pool to one's bedroom; in so many hotels this is a stifling route down corridors lined with blank doors. The entrance carved out of the ground and the covered ways of the centre at Piliyandala have the same aim and achieve a similar result.

It has been suggested that because so many of these examples deal with buildings related to tourism they are therefore of marginal interest to the development of architecture in Sri Lanka. This seems to me a mistaken view, not only because tourism is, despite its problems, an important economic consideration but mainly because an architecture catering to the foreign tourist encapsulates architectural issues which are general and not particular. Tourists come to enjoy the sea, the sun, the landscape and the celebrated monuments of the past. In one sense their presence and their needs intrude on and lessen exactly the values they have come to seek. Yet that is equally true in the case of Sri Lankans; they treasure the same values, while a growing population and an expanding economy – and all the construction which that implies – threaten a delicate landscape and a

170

fragile coastline. The important lesson which a number of Geoffrey Bawa's buildings demonstrate is that architecture can work with a landscape and not necessarily against it. This is certainly the case at the farm school, at the Serendip Hotel in Bentota, at Batujimbar in Bali, and it is shown again at the University of Ruhunu where terraces, retaining walls and buildings combine to make a hillside as unified as a sequence of stepped paddy fields.

It has also been said that a concern for architecture and any debate regarding appropriate models is altogether irrelevant in a country struggling to emerge from a period of serious underdevelopment. This charge again seems to me to totally misunderstand the needs of every country, whatever its state of development, as well as the value of architecture. We are all entitled to benefit from those celebrations which architecture makes possible and which are not only to be enjoyed by those able to have tea at the Taj. While teaching at Cambridge I often took visitors on an architectural tour of the colleges and the town. A sadly frequent remark made at the end of such a visit was that 'of course all this is fine and appropriate to the past but it has very little to do with the twentieth-century'; a remark which incidentally has immediate implications for model selection. My standard reply was that it may or may not be relevant to the twentieth century but I was certain it was crucial to the twenty-first century. Unless we are able to provide for everyone an environment as pleasurable, as meaningful and as treasured as that of Cambridge, we are failing both socially and architecturally. What is fundamentally important about the work of Geoffrey Bawa is that it shows that such an environment is possible and can be made relevant to us now.

Other architects in Sri Lanka have obviously felt this to be the case. The work of Bawa has become a model for others. That it has produced buildings seriously inferior to his own does not affect the way in which work becomes influential and meaningful or the way in which we use recent stock as a model. Part of the usefulness and visible appropriateness of these models comes, I suspect, in this instance from the cultural shift which has happened in the last decade or so and which ran parallel with Geoffrey Bawa's own changed use of the past.

20

The discussion of the buildings of Geoffrey Bawa covers the work of a considerable period and therefore deals largely with trends rather than specific instances. Unfortunately very little direct evidence is available on how the design process actually operates on a day-to-day basis within a design office or, most crucially, in the mind of an individual designer. Art historians have tried to assemble such evidence after the event and a few architects have occasionally described the antecedents of their design. Philip Johnson, for instance, did so in the case of his own house at New Canaan. The high premium on originality and the odium associated with copying, both of which have for long been a deep-seated assumption of current architectural practice, have probably worked against any exposition of sources as part of the description of an architectural project. I have therefore turned to one of my own projects as the third example. The following description of the design for the National Archaeological Museum of Jordan is an attempt to describe as many of the conscious architectural influences which were at work as could be remembered some time after the event. The influences affecting me were clearly modified by those at work on my collaborators. In addition there must have been other factors having an effect which could not be remembered later or which seemed so obvious, so much part of some natural process, that they remained unrecognised as

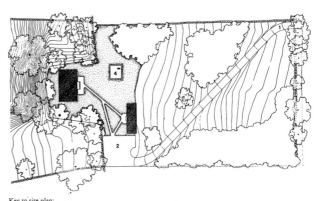

149 Philip Johnson
House at New Canaan, Conn. 1949
site plan

Key to site plan:
1. Entrance to site. 2. Car park. 3. Guest house. 4. Sculpture.
5. Glass house.

a distinctive feature. One possibly obvious factor is the view of the design process itself which assumes some briefing from a client, familiarity with the site, an association with consultants, or critical discussion with others working on the same project.

The commission to design the museum was the result of a limited competition organised by the Ministry of Tourism and Antiquities of the Hashemite Kingdom of Jordan among a number of British architects. One of the conditions was the establishment of a working association with an architectural office in Jordan. Such a link was made with Arabtech, a firm of architects, engineers and quantity surveyors in Amman. Buro Happold, structural and environmental engineering consultants in Bath, joined at the start of the competition and were chosen on the basis of experience in the Middle East and well-established personal and professional relations. The competition had been preceded by a report from Denis Haynes, at one time Keeper of Greek and Roman Antiquities at the British Museum, on the selection of a suitable site which recommended the Citadel in Amman as the best location.

The brief prepared by the Ministry indicated that a certain number of exhibits should be displayed but that new finds were continually being made and that there was therefore considerable uncertainty and an undoubted need for expansion. A limited number of elements were thus fixed at the outset: a client, a stated need, a site and a group of designers. There was no defined budget, only a maximum suggested size for the building.

Three members of the design team visited the site even before the results of the competition were known. It is a remarkable outcrop of stone rising above the centre of Amman, which is itself built on a number of hills. In the valley there is a sixth-century Roman amphitheatre, seating about 6000, which is in a fairly good state of repair. On the upper plateau of the citadel there are the remains of a Roman temple, a Byzantine church and an eighth-century Umayyad palace. In addition there are many earlier remains, some of which have been excavated and exposed. The citadel, however, had been put to other uses: the lower plateau was a playing field and occasional car park, the upper citadel had army huts, disused latrines, some workshops of the Archaeological

Service and a small existing museum. Visitors found their way among this casual accumulation, and families picnicked among the hollows and ridges which for part of the year turned remarkably green.

Even on the first visit to the site some thoughts about a possible location were unavoidable; some areas simply seemed more natural building ground than others. In particular the area following one of the upper contours curving round from the back of the existing museum towards the remains of the palace appeared obvious both in extent and place. This may have been influenced by the fact that it had derelict buildings on it already and therefore new building would be an improvement, as well as by the fact that a low building along the contours might be something like a castle wall and as a result in harmony with the existence of a citadel.

These attitudes to the site had been preceded by ideas about museums in general. I had been involved in museum and exhibition design for a number of years, had written two books and a number of articles, in the most recent of which I described the plan of the top floor of the Uffizi as perhaps an ideal form for a museum. I had become increasingly aware that the organisation of the visitor's route was a hallmark of museum design and that the solution at the Uffizi in Florence, where there was a primary route from which one could reach individual galleries, offered the greatest number of possibilities. The primary route, for instance, could take a number of different configurations without violating the princi-

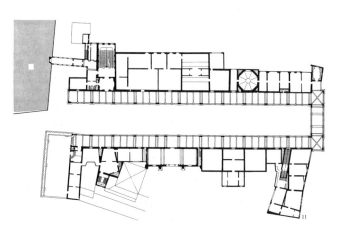

150 Giorgio Vasari
Uffizi, Florence, 1570
plan of top floor
(present arrangement by Ignazio Gardella, Giovanni Michelucci, Carlo Scarpa and Guido Morozzi, 1956)

ple; individual galleries could take on separate characteristics, as indeed happens at the Uffizi; a visitor could cut out those parts of the museum which he did not wish to see without having to go through all the galleries; the size of individual galleries could be varied without destroying the organisation of the building as a whole. I was determined that the museum on the citadel would follow this planning principle. It seemed particularly appropriate to a project which was likely to change during the design stage or possibly even during construction.

Ideas about siting were thus modified right at the start or at least directed along certain lines by quite general assumptions about appropriate organisation; there was a combination of notions about the individuality of the place and an almost abstract generality. This took on a slightly more defined form from the desire that the route within the museum building should form a component within a larger route which a visitor might take on the site as a whole; the building was thus likely to be linear and straddle a circuit between two definable points. A vague first sketch was possible.

This took the shape of a faceted crescent with three categories of space running parallel to each other: the inner ring was the primary circulation, the middle ring was the main galleries, and the outer and lower ring held stores and other servant spaces. The connection between these three lines occurred at the folds, the kind of punctuation of space by subsidiary elements associated with the plans of Louis Kahn. The diagram was probably more influenced by a recent visit to a very small exhibition area at the American Museum at Claverton near Bath where a collection of folk art was displayed in a crescent-shaped stable block. I was impressed by the awareness that a space gradually curving round only revealed itself progressively with the movement of the observer, an obvious fact which had also appealed to me many years ago when I first saw Frank Lloyd Wright's second residence for Herbert Jacobs and the first of his solar hemicycle houses and which I still remembered vividly. This unfolding of space seemed particularly appropriate to a museum display since it allowed concentration on a small area within which exhibits would be seen without losing sight of the building volume as a whole.

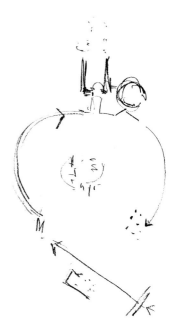

151 Michael Brawne and Associates
National Archaeological Museum,
Amman, Jordan, 1979–80
project, sketch of site and route

152 Michael Brawne and Associates
National Archaeological Museum,
Amman, Jordan, 1979–80
project, sketch plan – parallel spaces

153 Michael Brawne and Associates
National Archaeological Museum,
Amman, Jordan, 1979–80
project, sketch plan – fan
arrangement

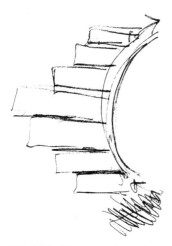

154 Michael Brawne and Associates
National Archaeological Museum,
Amman, Jordan, 1979–80
project, sketch of final plan

155 Alvar Aalto
Art Museum, Shiraz, Iran, 1970
project, site plan

Clearly, however, the diagram led to problems. The route was in a sense too dominant, too hierarchically equal with the galleries, and part of it would never be used properly since one would turn off it into a gallery at a fold line and only return to it at the next fold. Then the length of each gallery was fixed as the distance between two folds; not all the lengths need necessarily be equal, but this was geometrically odd and the possible variation was rather small. Also the number of galleries did not sensibly correspond to the divisions of the archaeological material; it was possible to increase the number but then the frequency of cranks would be excessive in relation to the whole. A considerable number of such alternatives was explored, the assumption being made that the various functions of the museum – display, storage, workshops, administration, restaurant – could all be subsumed within the diagrammatic layout.

One way out of the difficulty might be to produce a rather more fan-shaped plan where each gallery moved away centrifugally from the circulation ring. This seemed a much freer and more viable form if it could be made to work dimensionally. This however proved extremely difficult: the relative size of the elements really did not allow such a diagram. Actual magnitude obviously affects the appropriateness of a schematic arrangement.

The move from a tangential arrangement to a virtually radial one was the next step and one which in retrospect appears logical. It solved most of the problems of the earlier versions and incidentally came closest to the original intention of following the schema of the Uffizi. In a sense the first set of diagrams was a digression which probably came about from a preoccupation with the first impression formed on the citadel. The latest plan also owed something to Alvar Aalto's unbuilt project of 1970 for a museum at Shiraz in Iran and to a number of designs by Candilis, Josic and Woods which placed long rectangular spaces of various lengths parallel to each other. It did so not necessarily in an overt way, as in the case of the Uffizi, but simply because familiarity and a liking for those designs made certain solutions more acceptable than others. In neither instance, for example, was reference made to published plans, but simply to a conscious memory

176

of some features of a building. In the design process of recording ideas and then criticisng them it is likely that some answers suggested themselves more readily and survived more successfully because they related to the known stock of approved solutions.

The new plan of fingers stemming from a crescent did not immediately solve all problems and could not be expected to do so. The earlier design alternatives had in any case somewhat neglected the detailed planning of all the ancillary accommodation, which was nevertheless a sizeable proportion of the total. Now that a viable scheme seemed within sight, it was essential to study a greater number of aspects in more detail and to have preliminary talks about structure and services.

The relation of stores to galleries remained unsolved in the finger plan. The first thought was to put them below the galleries on the downhill side, rather as in the very first sketch. If the galleries were to expand this meant that the store should be a full floor lower in order to allow construction to extend above it. Because of the actual falls in the ground this was not always possible and was in any case a rather clumsy arrangement. Also no obvious routes down to storage arose out of the plan form; the feeling that this is a necessity belongs, of course, to a particular view of architecture in which order and differentiation are seen as important. From a closer study of the problem, it became clear that two quite different kinds of storage were needed: one area close to the service entrance for material being brought in from the archaeological digs to be cleaned, repaired, photographed, catalogued and so on, and another area for long-term storage of artefacts not on public view but available as a study collection.

A major service zone was therefore placed at the southern and lower end of the site and storage areas were provided within galleries at a mezzanine level. In other words, part of the storage space which might have been positioned below the galleries was put above them. Although this was a somewhat unusual location, it did not seem to involve any penalties which could not be overcome. On the contrary, when the preliminary drawings were made a number of advantages offered themselves. If a regular structural grid were to be used and this were to be placed over the site, with the galleries adjusting to the grid, then

156 Candilis, Josic and Woods Bochum University, Germany, 1963 project, view of model from the east

the mezzanine floors if joined to each other by a straight route would actually occupy different positions in each gallery. There would thus be an apparently logical rather than arbitrary difference in gallery layout or, perhaps more accurately, it would be possible to exploit the differences that occurred in terms of display. This was particularly the case not so much because of position but because the insertion of

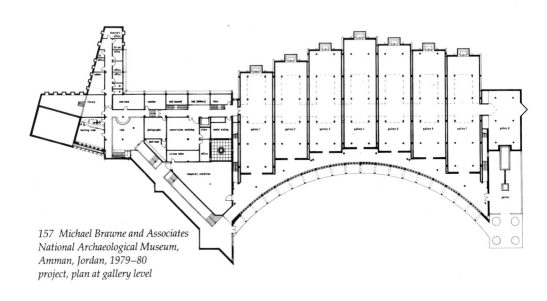

157 Michael Brawne and Associates
National Archaeological Museum,
Amman, Jordan, 1979–80
project, plan at gallery level

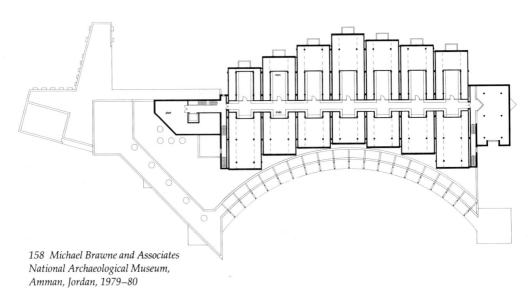

158 Michael Brawne and Associates
National Archaeological Museum,
Amman, Jordan, 1979–80
project, plan at study collection level

178

a mezzanine in the double-height space created a zone below the mezzanine floor which had a lower ceiling height and less natural light, and could therefore be treated differently. It seemed an obvious zone for the display of smaller objects, especially when these were in free-standing showcases. The greater control of illumination levels also made the area more appropriate for any material which might be damaged by excessive exposure to light.

The accommodation consisting of the storage space related to the service entry and the workshops, and thus in turn to administration, began to shape itself into some kind of entity which ought to be seen as separate from the organisation of the galleries. It was much more a blot than a line with off-shoots. There were also questions of geometric relationships with both the linear galleries and the existing structures, especially the remains of the Roman temple and the access road. A non-rectilinear geometry looked appropriate in resolving some of these difficulties, especially as it seemed rather more suggestive of the walls of a castle which had been shaped over the years on this hilltop. A literary and possibly romantic

159 Michael Brawne and Associates National Archaeological Museum, Amman, Jordan, 1979–80 project, view of central gallery

179

160 Michael Brawne and Associates
National Archaeological Museum,
Amman, Jordan, 1979–80
aerial view of model

connotation was actually pursued quite deliberately, and the way in which openings in walls were designed was intended to further this image.

There is no doubt that such a configuration of regular linear elements opposed to a more random set of spaces was influenced by two designs which had previously aroused my considerable interest and were thus highly acceptable models. The first was Hans Scharoun's State Library in Berlin, which in its plan form (if not in its elevations) I had always found fascinating and which suggested a geometry that was the result of a number of vectors deforming a space. The second was Reima Pietila's 'Dipoli' students' building at Otaniemi outside Helsinki, where regular rectangular spaces largely devoted to service functions were juxtaposed with flowing public spaces. It was exactly this *frisson* and complexity which was appealing, and which also looked as if it might solve specific and readily identifiable problems.

The sequence which can be recognised in the case of space planning is equally apparent in the development of structure and services. For example, the first document submitted at the very beginning of the competition suggested that a frame structure on point foundations would be most appropriate because it would create the least disturbance of the site and even allow the building to be raised above the ground so that excavations could still take place in the future. This decision stemmed not only from a desire to take account of the particular problems of the site but also from a knowledge that a frame structure was likely to be appropriate for a museum of this kind.

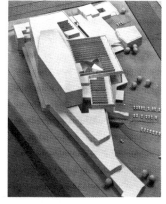

161 Hans Scharoun
State Library, Berlin, 1967–78
model seen from the north

180

162 *Reima Pietila and Raili Paatelainen*
'Dipoli' Student Centre, Institute of Technology, Otaniemi, Finland, 1966
plan of upper floor

The characteristics of the sequence became perhaps most obvious in the design of the environmental services. The climate of Amman shows considerable variation through the seasons as well as during the day. The winters are cool and wet – snow is not unknown – and the summers are hot and dry. Heating is certainly needed during the winter months; the summer temperatures suggest that special care ought to be taken in designing the enclosures, even if full air conditioning is not justified and is at present, in any case, not common. Few if any exhibits were made of organic material, so the requirements of conservation did not make very tight environmental control a necessity. It also seemed that atmospheric pollution which might affect stone and metal was not such that totally cleaned air was essential. The decision was therefore taken that the minimum amount of mechanical ventilation necessary for comfort should be used.

The first solution proposed mechanical ventilation from a central plant providing between six and eight air changes per hour. In the winter this air would be warmed, in the summer it would be at outside temperature. The critical period was the height of

181

summer, when outside temperatures were uncomfortable and to provide the same or higher temperatures indoors – because of lights, people and other gains – would do very little for body comfort. My view was that this solution was inappropriate on two counts: first, because in a museum where there were large volumes and relatively few people this number of air changes was not necessary; second, and most critically, it was counter to everyday practice and experience in the area. The normal routine was to close windows early in the day and not open them until late afternoon, in order to reduce the flow of air and thus trap the cool air of the night within the building. Although calculation and European assumptions pointed in one direction, local tradition pointed in quite another.

As soon as the concept of 'battening down' was established, a considerable number of design decisions were immediately made. Not only could the size of the mechanical plant and the related ductwork be reduced, but it became advantageous to increase the mass of the building in order to provide an adequate sink for storing the cool of the night. As a further source of cooling, it was also thought possible to use the ground and the air space which would exist below the building because of the sloping site. To

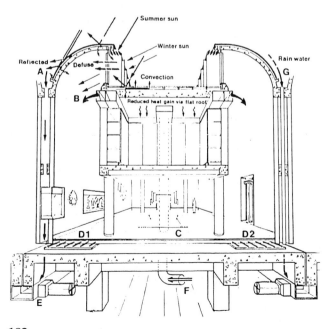

163 *Michael Brawne and Associates (Buro Happold Engineers) National Archaeological Museum, Amman, Jordan, 1979–80 project, section showing summer and winter environmental control arrangements*

182

make certain that the night air reached this zone, small fans were introduced to bring air down at night from the roof. It had previously been decided that the walls between the galleries would be double walls to allow recessed showcases, to provide space for gutters and to solve a visual problem of galleries as it were sliding past each other. It was now decided that the fans would bring the air down in this hollow space and thus 'wash' the partitioning walls with cool air. One design decision made in relation to a particular problem later provided solutions to other problems, and thus allowed the kind of meshing of answers which one often feels is analogous to elegance in mathematics.

The local authorities in Amman had encouraged us to store as much of the rainfall on the site as possible and to use it for watering the gardens in order to minimise our dependence on mains services. We therefore had to make provision for quite sizeable water reservoirs; clearly as many as possible should be placed in the cool zone below the building in order to increase still further the available mass. It also became obvious that this water could be circulated through the building in midsummer in order to cool the fabric and thus the air. A system was therefore designed whereby pipes embedded in the floor would be used for heating in the winter and cooling in the summer. They were in those parts of the gallery floor which were least likely to be obstructed by exhibits. Only a small amount of air was now needed to keep the rooms ventilated, and this could all be provided at high level from diffusers ringing the mezzanine enclosure.

The consultants devised a mathematical model of the building and of the environmental conditions. The results of these computer studies showed that the indoor temperature could be lowered significantly on the hottest days of the year, and that because of the flywheel effect of the building mass the indoor diurnal peak would not occur just after midday but would be postponed until the very late afternoon, by which time the museum would normally be closed to the public. The process of criticism in this case led to the amendment of the currently accepted solution towards a less normal system, itself rooted in earlier practice belonging to an empirical tradition and a less complex technology.

What was true of the design of the general planning and the engineering systems was very much repeated during the design of the building's details. In some instances, planning decisions were taken because they could be seen to be in line with specific predispositions towards solutions of small-scale construction. Prominent among these was an early decision that the building should be predominantly constructed out of stone and that, as a result, the solid to void ratio of the outside walls should be such that openings are obviously seen to be subsidiary.

The existence of earlier examples acting as models was equally pronounced. The entrance courtyard, a walled space with large gates, was from the start based on the kind of enclosure which might be found in a ruined castle; the carved stone panel above the main door was meant to reinforce this feeling. The paving divided by narrow channels in which there is flowing water was a direct imitation of the irrigation runnels at the Court of Oranges in front of what had been the Great Mosque in Seville, which I had seen and greatly admired many years ago. Similarly the small pools of water at hand height on either side of the entrance doors were a recollection of the water stairway in the gardens of the Generalife outside Granada, where one is able to trail one's hand in water flowing down the top of the balustrade. The fact that both examples come from Islamic gardens naturally seemed apposite; what was more important was that I knew and liked these designs and was thus predisposed towards them. For instance, I had used the idea of a water basin in which to cool one's hand at the entrance to the National Library of Sri Lanka in Colombo, where there were no Islamic precedents.

A major influence was undoubtedly the renaissance of museum design in Italy after World War II, exemplified most clearly by the work of Franco Albini, BBPR and Carlo Scarpa. The general attitudes to display developed by Italian architects of that period made their impact on a great many designers, and were a major theme of *The New Museum* which I wrote in 1963–65. These were by now widely accepted and most architects faced with this kind of a problem would have reacted towards them in some way. My own architectural emotions were most often aroused by some (though not all) examples of the work of Carlo Scarpa. This extended to aspects of display as well as to certain elaborations of detail and celebrations of small functional necessities like the protection of vulnerable corners of buildings or the placement of even a matwell.

Scarpa himself undoubtedly owed a great deal to Frank Lloyd Wright and Charles Rennie Mackintosh;

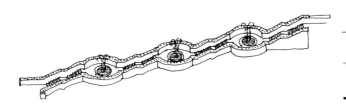

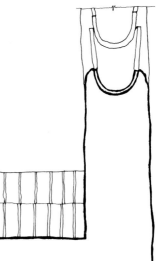

164 *Generalife, Granada, Spain*
the water stairway

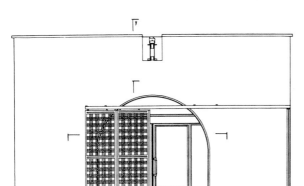

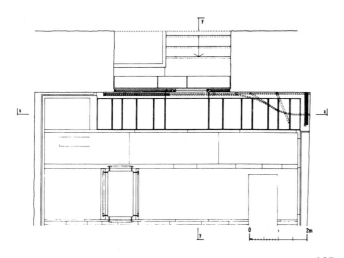

165 *Carlo Scarpa*
Castelvecchio Museum, Verona,
1956–64
elevation and plan of ground floor
exit door measured drawing by
Richard Murphy

185

his acknowlededement of Wright was particularly obvious and open. He also belonged to a long-standing Italian tradition of craftsmanship in which the joy of making things is especially apparent. A great many building objects are still made by hand in Amman, and the craft of working in stone and marble is still alive. It was appropriate therefore to detail display supports or seats or the surrounds of openings so that these skills were used and added to the visual and tactile sensations of a visitor.

The most crucial considerations revolved around the design of the lighting; it is through light that a museum's objects are made visible, so its control is inevitably a vital design decision. From the very beginning any notion of putting the objects in dark spaces and lighting them entirely artificially was rejected. It went counter to my visual preferences,

166 *Carlo Scarpa*
Castelvecchio Museum, Verona,
1956–64
view of entrance to sculpture gallery

made relationships with the outside and particularly the existing archaeological remains impossible, and was in any case unnecessary since hardly any of the objects in the collection were sensitive to light. Conversely, a totally glazed enclosure was not only climatically unsuitable but made display very difficult since the eye did not know whether to focus on the exhibit or the landscape. Enough examples of both these extremes were in existence and sufficiently known to make an early rejection possible. The desirable prototypes were rooms which allowed some outlook and were lit in such a way that the quality of natural light could be sensed while the source itself was not obvious.

Historically the most evolved examples were the baroque and rococo churches of southern Germany. More recently, some of the buildings by Aalto showed similar design traits and were perhaps most exuberant in the museum at Aalborg by Alvar and Elissa Aalto and Jean-Jacques Baruel. When I saw the building late in 1972 I had been impressed by the flamboyance and sculptural expressiveness of the section in the central gallery for temporary exhibitions, but felt equally strongly that these forms controlling light were overwhelming the space and the works of art. A more subdued solution seemed right, particularly one in which most of the light was reflected off surfaces so that it was diffused and the brilliance of the source could be shielded.

The half-barrel vault which was eventually evolved appeared to answer in the most direct way the criteria which were partly stated, partly assumed. The fact

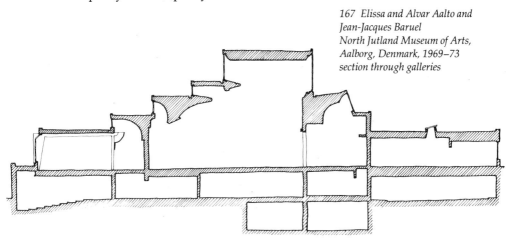

167 Elissa and Alvar Aalto and Jean-Jacques Baruel
North Jutland Museum of Arts, Aalborg, Denmark, 1969–73
section through galleries

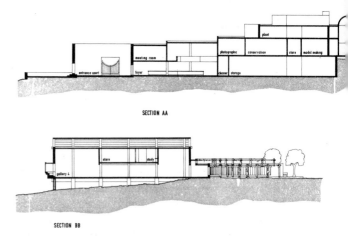

SECTION AA

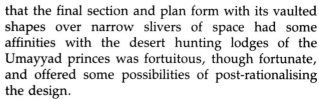

SECTION BB

that the final section and plan form with its vaulted shapes over narrow slivers of space had some affinities with the desert hunting lodges of the Umayyad princes was fortuitous, though fortunate, and offered some possibilities of post-rationalising the design.

Side-lighting also needed control. This could be achieved in a number of ways, but two were pursued with greater interest than any others.

The distinguishing marks of current architecture in Amman are few. In most instances buildings are sensibly low and faced in stone so that the hillsides remain an agglomeration of reasonably small and similar units which do not overwhelm the shape of the ground. At the finer scale what becomes noticeable is the frequent use of pergolas, which provide outdoor shaded spaces and also shade windows during the summer. This lightly framed architecture over which a partly disordered vegetation grew was highly appealing; it rhymed with an enthusiasm for pergolas which had been strongly reinforced some years previously when I first came across Schinkel's watercolours of his design for Orianda, the palace in the Crimea, while designing the Age of Neo-Classicism exhibition in 1972. Pergolas provided a transition between building and landscape in which one form poured, as it were, over the other to make a zone in which both were happily at home. Such a solution looked entirely appropriate for the open side of the crescent which curved around the hollow centre of the site.

169 Qusayr Amra, Jordan, circa 715
exterior of the baths

170 Karl Friedrich Schinkel
Palace at Orianda, Crimea, 1838
project, view of Imperial Garden
Court

188

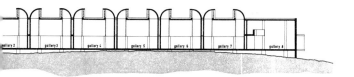

The other method of light control which appeared obvious and was explored was that of fine grilles. This was a long-standing Islamic tradition related to light control as well as the needs of privacy where women were concerned. Many parts of the Islamic world contain wonderful examples of grilles in wood, marble or stone. The problem here was that grilles ought also to make openings burglar-proof. Two kinds were devised in metal: one for office windows, where there were also adjustable shutters or blinds which would reduce the incoming light and which could therefore be made of rods and be reasonably far apart, the second for gallery windows, which were egg crates providing more permanent sun and light control and which were much closer in that sense to

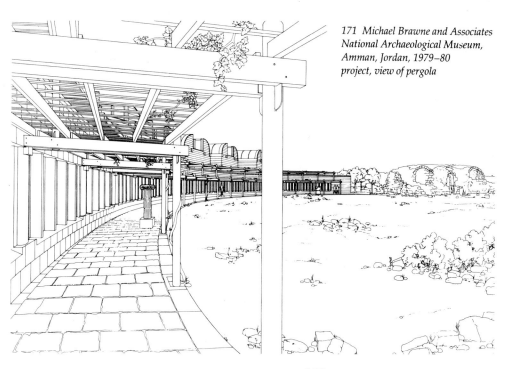

171 *Michael Brawne and Associates National Archaeological Museum, Amman, Jordan, 1979–80 project, view of pergola*

172 Hassan Fathy
Samy House, Dashure, Egypt, 1979
mashrabiyya in master bedroom

the traditional window screen, the mashrabiyya, of open squares so often found in Egypt, for example.

In both these instances the references to earlier examples were very conscious, and attempts were made to find sources in the form of illustrations or actual buildings. During excursions from Amman to Jerusalem and Damascus, for example, we were continually on the lookout for precedents which could be said to belong to a regional building tradition. In each case the vocabulary we had developed was enriched or modified. Although the grilles and pergolas are in no way identical with any we saw, their design was undoubtedly influenced and, critically, directed to a certain range of answers because references were made to existing solutions which were perceived as models.

This description of part of the design process of a particular building is, needless to say, greatly simplified and quite deliberately emphasises one particular side of that process. It says hardly anything at all about the role of the client, the need to meet deadlines of presentation, the impact of the actual process of drawing, or the effect of discussions with associates and the differences of opinion which arise from different visual predilections or different attitudes to the design process. All serious attempts to monitor in some scientific way the many highly complex interweavings of design have, so far, been unsuccessful or have produced rather trivial findings. In this case there has simply been an attempt to describe from memory the interaction between two aspects: the selective awareness of the existing stock of solutions and the final building design.

21

The way decisions are made about structure and environmental services was discussed briefly in the description of the National Archaeological Museum in Jordan; it is nevertheless true to say that the bulk of this essay has not concerned itself with the technical aspects of building. This is not intended to imply that the way we make design decisions on constructional matters differs significantly from those on formal matters. The two are in any case so closely entwined that it would be hard to approach them separately. The emphasis on form arose from a belief that it is more obvious, more readily understood; that in a sense it is more visible and therefore more easily related to everyday experience. It might also be said that the technological considerations of architecture are closer to science than the formal ones, so it would not be surprising if the process of thought and application were akin to some scientific method. I would argue that the experience of practice suggests that the way we approach the various aspects of architecture is remarkably similar, and that constructional design again follows a $P_1 \rightarrow TS \rightarrow EE \rightarrow P_2$ sequence.

The window, to take an example, is an important part of any building and presents considerable technical difficulties. It is a significant interruption of the wall plane. Most constructional problems occur at the junction of different components: there is likely to be a change of materials, a relation between elements having different constructional tolerances, coefficients of expansion or simply weathering properties. These problems are compounded in the window by the necessity to move some part of it when ventilation is needed.

In 1958 I was designing my own house in London and anxious, from both choice and necessity, to produce a simple and highly economical solution. I had recently returned to England from the USA (where I had lived in a timber house by Bernard Maybeck) and was interested in curtain walling, then still a somewhat innovatory construction, but was also strongly influenced by such combinations of timber and brick as Aalto had used in the library wing of the town hall at Säynätsalo. Cost made the use of softwood inevitable, and the problem was therefore, in terms of the task I had set myself, how to create an assembly of timber and glass which could fit within the planes of brickwork.

The visual effect of curtain walling is one of precision and of sharp rectangular components. I was keen to replicate something of the same character in timber, particularly when seen from the outside. The normal method of placing glass into timber frames was then to use putty or beads externally. Putty demands painting, and in this design I was intent on using timber which was treated only with wood preservative, partly for reasons of simpler and less expensive maintenance, partly because wood preservatives do not obscure the grain of the wood; an exposure of the natural materials – timber, unplastered brickwork – was very much part of the chosen visual vocabulary, which itself was part of the prevalent style.

The actual method of detailing which was eventually chosen was to insert the glass so that at the top and sides it fitted into rebates which had beads on the inside set in mastic, but at the bottom the rebate faced outwards and the timber bead would therefore also be on the outside. This seemed to make sense in terms of water exclusion. All beads had square outlines in keeping with the notion of sharp profiles. Very soon, however, the water which tended to settle on the flat top of the bottom beads began to damage these and the adjacent mastic bedding; the windows leaked at the bottom. Remedial action – error elimination – was necessary; a polysulphide mastic (more effective but also more expensive) was substituted, and the tops of the bottom beads were

173 Alvar Aalto
Town Hall, Säynätsalo, Finland,
1950–52
south elevation

192

chamfered so that there was a slope which would throw the water away – a return to a traditional detail.

Six years later I designed a house in Hampshire overlooking a small lake. For reasons very similar to those which determined choices on the London house, timber windows seemed again to be appropriate, but I was now at the P_2 stage of the design sequence. The specification of the timber was changed from ordinary softwood to western red cedar. This has a lower strength, which meant smaller panes of glass, a fact I quite welcomed since it produced a denser mesh of timber lines on the elevation. In my own house the effect was perhaps a little too open. The most important amendment was

175 Michael Brawne
Own house, Hampstead, London,
1958
interior at night

193

176 Michael Brawne
House at Fisher's Pond, Hampshire,
1964
plan

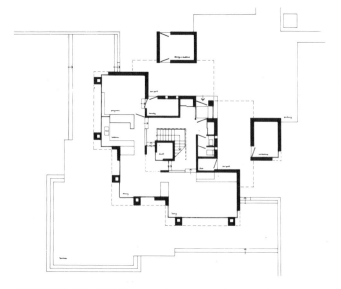

177 Michael Brawne
House at Fisher's Pond, Hampshire,
1964
view from north-west

178 Michael Brawne
House at Fisher's Pond, Hampshire,
1964
corner

to omit the troublesome bottom timber glazing bead altogether and to substitute a flat aluminium section only 3 mm thick. This created a minimal ledge and the material was rot-proof.

The house in London had glass louvres for ventilation. I believed these to be effective, and they could also be recessed into the mullions to produce the least visual interruption to the rhythm of the façade. It was difficult to make them completely airtight and I therefore changed, on the Hampshire house, to the use of casements. This was to some extent also prompted by the fact that louvres had become commonplace for lavatories and other ante-room windows; they had been devalued, or perhaps more correctly, they tended to carry unacceptable connotations.

194

In order to protect the timber in general, the whole exterior was designed so that at each horizontal junction in the construction there was also a step inwards; the building skin was like a series of fish scales. This had immediate visual implications, which were exploited so that the house could be 'read' as a set of horizontal layers, the upper always overhanging the lower.

P_3 introduced new aspects into the problem. The design was for a Physics Laboratory on a site at Egham in Surrey for Royal Holloway College, part of the University of London, and was started in 1972. The building was to be clad in Cor-Ten steel, a material which I found extremely interesting because it combined the qualities of a metal with the kind of patina of weathering associated with stone. Cor-Ten is a steel alloy which in the normal weather cycle of wet and dry periods forms a layer of rust; this eventually adheres to the parent metal and thus produces a coating which prevents further oxidation. Because Cor-Ten must not remain wet for long periods, ledges are again to be avoided.

The important new requirement was for flexibility in room arrangement and the possibility of future change. I decided that the subdivision of the fenestration could be random, in effect somewhat like the mullion spacing at Le Corbusier's refectory at La Tourette. Each mullion would be wide enough to take the end of a partition. The band of windows on each floor would be detailed so that it consisted of a top and bottom rail, with the possibility of fixing mullions

179 Michael Brawne and Associates Tolansky Laboratory, Royal Holloway and Bedford New College, Egham, Surrey, 1973–74 south-west corner

180 Michael Brawne and Associates Tolansky Laboratory, Royal Holloway and Bedford New College, Egham, Surrey, 1973–74 east elevation

195

at any point along that rail. These rails would also be used to hold the glass while the mullions held the sides of the louvres, to which I returned for financial reasons. In order to avoid a bottom ledge, the glass was supported along its lower edge by two clips secured to the bottom rail, a 'Unistrut' channel which

Key

1. mastic asphalt on sheathing felt over 25 mm insulation board and 50 mm metal decking
2. 12-gauge Cor-Ten capping and fixing straps
3. 178 × 102 × 21.6 mm steel I-beam
4. 12-gauge Cor-Ten on roofing felt over 50 mm high-density woodwool slabs and pvc vapour barrier
5. softwood rail
6. 162 × 76.2 mm ms angle with gusset stiffners
7. Venetian blind
8. 40 × 45 mm hardwood top fixing rail
9. 12 mm blockboard
10. one-hour resistant casing to columns in canvas reinfroced vermiculite plaster
11. 32oz glass
12. 9 mm external quality plywood sill
13. 40 × 40 mm unistrut channel
14. 127 × 64 mm rolled steel channel
15. 3.5 mm hardboard fixed to softwood framing
16. 20 mm chipboard convector fascia
17. unistrut clip to hold glass
18. underscreed trunking
19. vinyl tiles
20. 60 mm screed
21. Cor-Ten dressed down to form drip
22. neoprene gasket
23. 152.4 × 16.24 mm rolled hollow steel section
24. 3 mm plywood cover strip
25. hardwood coverstrip
26. precast sill
27. 100 mm lignacite semi-solid
28. metric brickwork
29. dpc dressed down to foundation beam

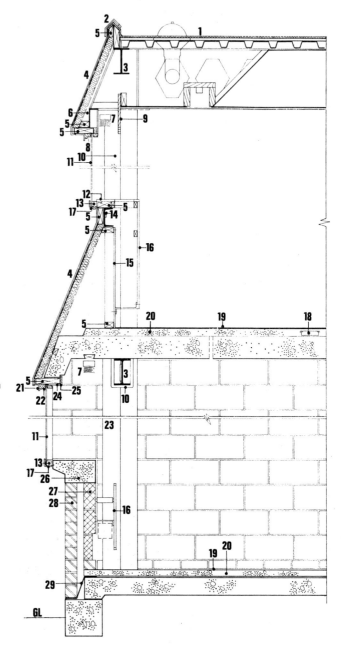

181 Michael Brawne and Associates Tolansky Laboratory, Royal Holloway and Bedford New College, Egham, Surrey, 1973–74 typical section through outside wall

196

holds a nut anywhere along its length into which a bolt can be fixed. If the position of the partitions needed to be altered, the mullions could be re-arranged and at most a new sheet of glass would be required. The solution was very much a development of the earlier constructions.

The design of the National Library of Sri Lanka, begun in 1975, was a return to the ideas worked out on the house in Hampshire. Overhangs seemed to solve two of the most serious environmental prob-lems of Colombo: sun and heavy rain. The climate is such that, given shade and protection from rainfall, one is as comfortable in the open throughout the year as is possible without mechanical means; the building was therefore conceived as a series of open trays under a large umbrella. Each floor projected beyond the lower one and the roof projected beyond the top floor so that the section was, from top to bottom, a protecting sequence of inward steps. This shielding made it possible to adopt on a multi-storey building the traditional arrangement by which a band between the ceiling and the top of the window consists of a series of slats without any intermediate glazing. Ventilation is the primary requirement in the humid tropics so that the skin is cooled by latent heat of evaporation.

Windows were made of hardwood, a local mate-rial, and consisted of a series of hinged casements so as to provide the maximum opening. Alternate pairs

182 Michael Brawne
National Library of Sri Lanka,
Colombo, completed 1990
cross-section

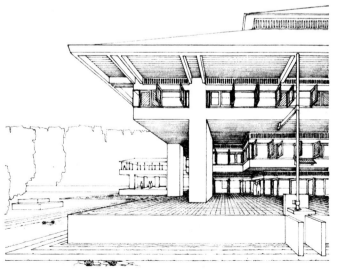

183 Michael Brawne
National Library of Sri Lanka,
Colombo
presentation perspective, 1975

197

184 *Michael Brawne*
National Library of Sri Lanka,
Colombo, completed 1990
south-west corner

of casements were designed to have a solid infill so that when open they provided lateral shading from the low east and west sun. The profiles of all the timber sections were kept simple so that they could be made easily with the available techniques; weatherproofness did not really matter since the sequence of overhangs provided adequate protection.

I believe this series of examples, or any comparable series, shows that the technical and formal aspects of design are very similar and highly intertwined. If we accept the traditional model as satisfactory we are following the routine solution, which has already presumably gone through the TS → EE sequence at earlier periods. If for some reason we depart from that, whether because other techniques have become available or other visual effects are wanted, we presumably start at P_1 and may then go through a P_1, P_2 . . . series. The examples just discussed also point out the degree to which personal preferences are important, and how these may limit problem recognition and the array of models likely to be selected. The importance given to mullions, for instance, goes through all the designs.

A short while after I had finished drawing the detailed section of the National Library, I saw Geoffrey Bawa's hotel at Bentota on the coast south of Colombo. Its section also consisted of a sequence of projecting floors with a large roof overhang; the similarity was immediately obvious and almost worrying. The building had not at that time been

185 *Geoffrey Bawa*
Bentota Beach Hotel, Bentota, Sri Lanka, 1969

198

published, although it has since been illustrated widely, so I could not have been aware of it as a precedent. Nor are other buildings in the tropics quite like that. The occurrence of similar solutions or inventions almost simultaneously or within a very short period, frequent in both art and science, seems to stem from a common problem recognition at a particular time. It is often abetted by the opportunities of some new technical means – in this case reinforced concrete, which had not been used previously on a large scale in Sri Lanka and which made possible the kind of cantilever construction used in both these buildings.

The idea of a *Zeitgeist* plays a significant role in some views of history but poses considerable difficulties, since in the last resort actions are performed by individuals with at least a limited set of choices. It may really be no more than a narrowing of the spectrum of problems, with a corresponding limitation in the number of acceptable models. In retrospect and using our knowledge of history we also tend to measure the plausibility of past events and their likely date by the degree to which they conform to the known contemporary models. This applies as much to architecture as it does to social or political history.

22

186 *Villard de Honnecourt*
Sketchbook
Tower of Laon Cathedral

187 *Leonardo da Vinci*
sketches for centralised churches

In the examples just discussed, the sequence P_1 through to P_2 was considered as a long-term cycle in which both the first and second problems were buildings. The intermediate stages of a tentative solution and its error eliminations were in the form of drawings or occasionally scale models. The most frequent cycle in architecture, however, is a short-term one in which both P_1 and P_2 are drawings and TS and EE are iterated until a solution survives the last set of tests or there is no more time in which to carry out further refutations.

The architectural drawing stands as an analogue for the real building. It is drawn according to a set of recognised coventions which allow it to be used as a means of communication; the more messages the drawing has to transmit to others, the more emphasis there is on a rigorous observance of those conventions. An architect's quick sketches as part of his own exploration of a problem are personal and may only loosely follow the accepted rules; a drawing intended as an instruction for use on the site has to be entirely unambiguous, and it normally achieves this by an adherence to the known methods and symbols.

The two key conventions presuppose horizontal or vertical cuts through a building. Both plan and section are abstractions which do not correspond to the way in which a building is actually perceived. The plan in particular assumes a bird's eye view of the whole building, whereas the eye actually sees spaces one at a time and at right angles to the view drawn on plan. Nevertheless our memories are sufficiently stored with models that we believe that we can visualise these abstractions as built realities. A considerable part of a designer's expertise lies precisely in this ability, since such skill is essential in the TS and EE sequence performed by means of drawings.

A glance at work in progress in an office will immediately reveal that most preparatory drawings are a mixture of more or less carefully drawn plans and sections combined with, often indeed crowded out by, small sketches of details or perspective views. These visual notes are a continuous set of tests of what is being drawn more conventionally. This

188 Carlo Scarpa
Castelvecchio Museum, Verona,
1956
drawing of final design for the
suppport of the Cangrande statue

combination of graphic techniques has been used by designers for centuries: examples can be found in Villard de Honnecourt's thirteenth-century sketchbook, they abound in Leonardo da Vinci's notebooks of the fifteenth century, and Carlo Scarpa's published drawings show a dense overlay of architectural explorations interrupted occasionally by figures of women or ironic self-portraits.

Architectural students soon acquire the habit, and in fact most conversations between student and teacher are a dual communication of words and quick drawings which test the student's proposals or explore the suggestions being made as resolutions of some problem. The sketches record the iconic thinking in messages which can be transmitted. Both conjecture and refutation take the form of drawings.

It must be admitted that what we draw is influenced by the models which were the starting point of the design, to the extent that we frequently draw what we would like to see rather than what the conventions strictly demand should be drawn.

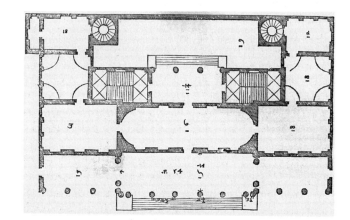

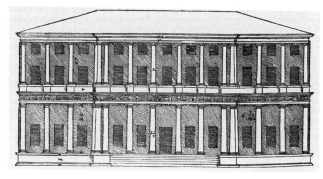

189 Andrea Palladio
Palazzo Chiericati, Vincenza, 1550
drawing from 'Quattro Libri' Venice,
1570

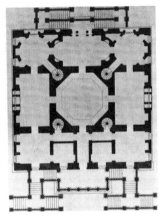

190 *Andrea Palladio*
Palazzo Chiericati, Vincenza, 1550
contemporary photograph

Palladio, for example, illustrating the Palazzo Chiericati in his *Quattro Libri*, does so as if the columns are free-standing and the whole wall plane is set well back, creating a colonnade. In fact the wall above the centre of the loggia is set between the columns. It is thought that Palladio 'visualised its façade in terms of a Roman forum' and therefore drew it so that it resembled its antique prototype. When Lord Burlington designed Chiswick House in about 1725 he had Palladio's Villa Rotonda of 1565 clearly in his mind as the example to follow. The plan of Chiswick House shows the location of fireplaces quite specifically in the outer walls of rooms; the elevations fail to show any chimneys, just as the Villa Rotonda does not show any flues. Only a later engraving by J. Roque in 1736 indicates how very obvious the chimneys are at Chiswick and how very much they are part of our perception of the house.

Whatever the effect of these occasional misrepresentations, the point I wish to emphasise is that both the end-product (the building) and the process of communication and testing (the drawings) are each firmly rooted in visual concepts. This may seem like an entirely banal statement. However, it ought to be remembered that structural engineering, which is just as much concerned with the making of forms seen in space, gives primacy to mathematical calculations. What I take to be crucial, and of importance outside the field of visual design, is the fact that in architecture the process of design uses the closest possible analogue to the eventual building. The entire P_1 and P_2 sequence remains internally coherent.

191 *Lord Burlington*
Chiswick House, London, c.1725
ground floor plan

192 *Lord Burlington*
Chiswick House, London, c.1725
engraving of south front, 1727

193 *Andrea Palladio*
Villa Rotonda, Vincenza, 1565–66
engraving

203

194 J. Roque
Chiswick Villa
engraving, 1736

The drawing must of necessity represent a static view of the building; in addition to visualising volumes in their reality we must therefore somehow imagine our kinaesthetic experience of the designed space. I believe that one of the important aspects of perspective – particularly perspective with a single vanishing point, as in the drawings and paintings of the fifteenth and sixteenth centuries in Italy – is that it allows us somehow to imagine travelling through a spatial sequence towards the vanishing point. One of the significant contributions of computer-aided design (CAD) has been the development of programs which allow us to view a building in perspective, and to have it rotated and, even more important, to have movement towards it and through its interior simulated. CAD allows us to carry out a test which has greater verisimilitude than is possible with traditional drawings. Although the program has a mathematical basis, the simulation is still visual.

It is generally only after the whole range of tentative solutions and error elimination processes has been completed that a serious attempt is made to produce a quite different set of drawings, namely documents which are instructions to a contractor to build in a specific way to achieve the previously determined outcome. Tentative constructional drawings – explorations of methods of building and of appropriate details of structure, services and the relation between these – are an integral part of the iterative process of design. Documents to a builder,

195 Pisanello
drawing of interior

204

however, have legal, contractual implications and are instructions for the performance of tasks using defined materials. These documents are partly in a written form – usually specifications and Bills of Quantities – but largely in the form of detailed drawings which could be described as anatomical dissections of a building. They show both the components and the assembly, either together or separately.

In order for the instructions to be as unambiguous as possible it is necessary for these drawings to have the fullest relevant information and to be drawn using the accepted conventions so that their legibility is not in doubt. A great deal of time and effort is therefore expended on them, and it could be said that some of the craft aspects of architecture – in the sense that a writer uses his craft to make his sentences flow – are deployed in the preparation of such instructional material. The visual character of the final drawings differs considerably from that of the earlier exploratory probings.

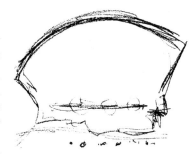

196 Michael Brawne and Associates Student's Union, Royal Holloway and Bedford New College, Egham, Surrey, 1985–86, sketch

197 Michael Brawne and Associates Student's Union, Royal Holloway and Bedford New College, Egham, Surrey, 1985–86 presentation drawings, plans

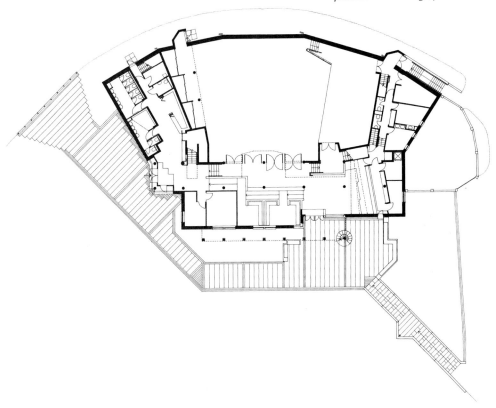

*198 Michael Brawne and Associates
Student's Union, Royal Holloway
and Bedford New College, Egham,
Surrey, 1985–86
constructional drawing, plan*

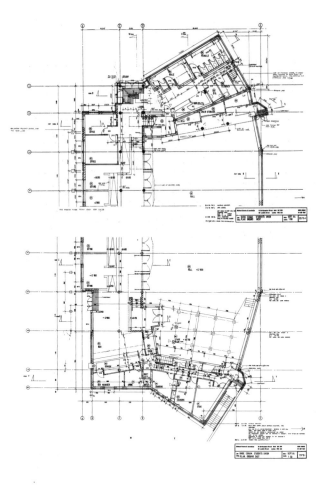

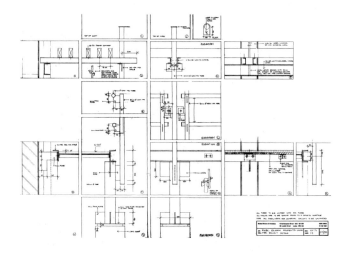

*199 Michael Brawne and Associates
Student's Union, Royal Holloway
and Bedford New College, Egham,
Surrey, 1985–86
constructional drawing of balcony*

206

200 *Michael Brawne and Associates Student's Union, Royal Holloway and Bedford New College, Egham, Surrey, 1985–86 view of completed balcony*

If we compare an early sketch, a presentation drawing and the constructional drawing for the Students' Union building at Royal Holloway and Bedford New College, for instance, each only showing the ground floor plan, the differences become obvious. At one level the information content of the constructional drawing, and thus its visual density, is much higher. At another level it is less of an analogue of the eventual building because it contains information which cannot be sensed by an observer of the completed construction; it could be said to be less 'true'. This is the case not only when dealing with the more abstract concept of the plan but equally when drawing an elevation or the details of something like an obvious, almost sculptural element such as a balcony.

What preceded the constructional drawing in this case was a long process which included questions of the convenience, indeed the very possibility, of making the visual effect, and its relation to other parts of the building and to its immediate neighbour designed the year before – and of course to the visual language, the preferred expression, which had governed the design of these buildings.

Both the Student's Union and its earlier neighbour, a physics research building, had discernible models,

207

201 *Michael Brawne and Associates Wilson Laboratory, Royal Holloway and Bedford New College, Egham, Surrey, 1985–86 view from south-west*

the choice of which was not arbitrary or based on preferences unrelated to the uses of the building. In the case of the physics building the spaces had to consist of laboratories, offices and seminar rooms – each self-contained, each specific to some purpose and each probably best as a simple cubicular volume. The same was true of the even earlier physics teaching building, where the influence of Kahn and particularly of his Bryn Mawr dormitories is evident in the notion of a diagonal symmetry and the extension of a building by attachment at the corner; through making point contact we disturb the existing building least when a new one has to be grafted on.

The spaces of the Union building did not need to be self-contained, nor did many have a reason to be cubicular. On the contrary, the flow of space like the movement of people within the building suggested continuity rather than boundaries. The shape of the site on the bend of the road also led naturally to a non-rectangular geometry. One of the most obvious precedents for such spatial fluidity and non-orthogonal spaces lies in the work of Alvar Aalto.

It could therefore be said that the selection of a model for the two physics laboratories and for the Students' Union was a combination of function and preference. It could also be said that the model shift which occurred when the Union was designed stemmed from a recognition that the nature of the problem had altered. Yet the three buildings have a certain similarity because they originate from the same hand, and they differ markedly from quite functionally similar science buildings done at the

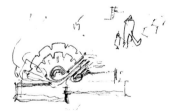

205 *Alvar Aalto Library, Rovaniemi, 1963 design sketch, plan*

208

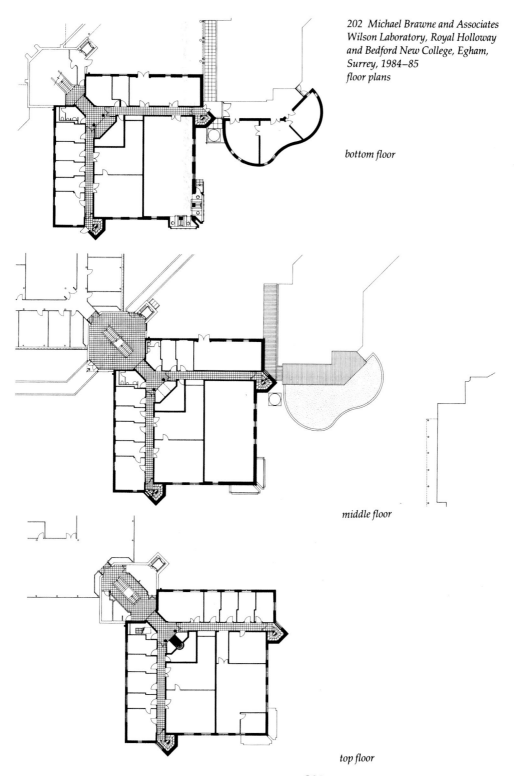

202 *Michael Brawne and Associates*
Wilson Laboratory, Royal Holloway
and Bedford New College, Egham,
Surrey, 1984–85
floor plans

bottom floor

middle floor

top floor

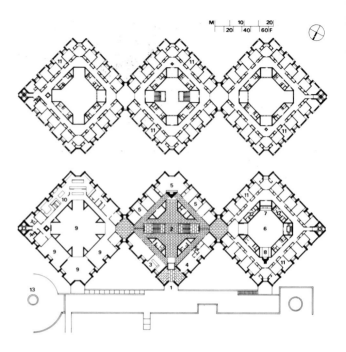

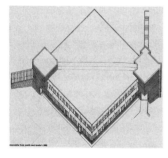

204 Michael Brawne and Associates
Tolansky Laboratory, Royal
Holloway and Bedford New College,
Egham, Surrey, 1973–74
axonometric showing point
connections

same time as part of the development of the site by other architects. Their designs were rooted in other models.

Yet if one looked at the constructional drawings for these other and dissimilar buildings it is virtually certain that the methods of recording and transmitting the necessary instructions would be found to be practically identical. The process of design is individual, even though it may very frequently have recourse to a model as its starting point, but in architecture the translation of that design is done by others who need 'neutral' instructions. These might even take the form of numerical codes standing for particular components. The work of the designer, intent on creating a future artefact, is dependent on another agency whose means are not strictly within the visual sequence which can be established as an internally consistent line for the design process. There is, as it were, a period of discontinuity during the construction process, even when some decisions about the eventual building are made on the site.

It is not until the building is complete, and we are able to experience it visually and kinaesthetically, that we return to the visual realm in which the design process expressed itself. The completed building is

210

also, as I suspect most designers would admit, both less and more than had been imagined; less because expectations are seldom entirely fulfilled, more because chance effects and unexpected combinations produce new results. In the design sequence, however experienced and skilful we may be, we are not dealing with the real object but with some analogue, so reality has inevitably some surprises. And these new realisations will affect our perception of the next problem.

Perspective

23

The design of buildings is only one of a number of design processes which lead to the making of some artefact. Because of the complexity of architecture and its symbolic values – because of its higher content – design as a conscious activity has been acknowledged in architecture for several thousand years. Vitruvius's treatise alone is sufficient proof. The number of objects which are deliberately designed rather than the result of a traditional craft system has increased enormously, however. It is likely that at least 95% of the environment in which this page is being read has in some large measure been designed. That applies right through from the building to the typeface image on the paper. If Popper's hypothetico-deductive method is relevant to architecture, and especially if the P_1 to P_2 sequence is an accurate description of the design process as actually performed, it can surely be argued that this method is likely to have an extremely wide application throughout the design tasks which lead to the making of so much of our surroundings.

Design seen as a general activity has something to do with the deliberate consideration of some outcome, with the forecast and control of some future event. It is always in some measure a prognosis, and because it is likely to affect more than just the designer it raises social and moral issues. If design were to start from some absolute rational basis (supposing that could be achieved) it is highly likely that the experience of the past would be neglected, and that there would be a considerable mismatch between society's recognition of a current problem and the designer's answer. In the political arena, as so many societies have been painfully aware, this often leads to the imposition of solutions by dictatorial means in the name of some future benefit, of tomorrow's utopia.

The deliberate controlled forecast of a future outcome, thought of in the widest sense, is an activity which is performed in a considerable range of endeavours; it does not only apply when the outcome is an artefact. The range extends from tomorrow's dinner party to the government's annual budget. The difficulties of applying a design sequence which in some way parallels that in visual design is that in most instances it is much more difficult or even impossible to achieve the kind of internal consistency which occurs through the use of drawings. In the case of the dinner party it is quite likely that we play safe and avoid tentative solutions; we use a known and previously successful menu and cook the meal by the accepted craft methods. The outcome, at least in the culinary sense, has a high probability of success. The probability is sure to be much lower in the case of the budget, and in any case a match between plan and achievement may be due to chance.

Recent studies in economic planning have concerned themselves with such difficulties and have led to the development of econometric models; these attempt to simulate through mathematical models the workings of the economy so that tentative solutions and error eliminations can be performed with the greatest possible level of internal consistency and therefore presumably with a greater measure of success. The aim must be to achieve the highest attainable level of correspondence between model and reality.

Verbal descriptions and discussions can never achieve high levels of correspondence. Language may be the only effective means of argument, but it lacks that internal coherence with the wide spectrum of design activity which makes the analogic model so powerful. Even in language where TS and EE are of crucial significance, as in logic, there is a drive to invent and use non-verbal symbols which can be said to have internal consistency. The great importance of the computer in intellectual and social terms is that it makes possible the development of a varied range of models, and we are then able to apply to these models rapid sequences of alternative solutions and their error elimination. This suggests that we are increasingly likely to apply the design method which has been in use in architecture for centuries to the widest possible range of activities.

24

Henry Ford's often quoted aphorism that 'history is bunk' would seem to be both inaccurate and inapplicable to the design and manufacture of motor cars. Ford was not the inventor of the automobile and, significantly, it is difficult to make an attribution for the invention to a single person. The car was very much a gradual development of the 'horseless carriage'. Similarly Ford's use of the assembly line was by no means original but was derived from principles applied in other areas of mechanisation, particularly earlier forms of industrialisation such as grain milling or yarn spinning. The history of mechanical inventions, which Giedion and others have documented fully, shows quite clearly that most innovation takes the form of adapting an existing model. One of the early attempts to mechanise the cutting of corn, for example, was a British patent taken out in 1811 which shows a blade, like a circular saw, fixed to the front of a two-wheeled cart. The horses are harnessed to the back of the cart so that they push the rotating blade in front of them, thus imitating the action of a reaper with a scythe. It was not until later that the cutting action became more like that of scissors and moved to the side and back of the horses.

One of the clearest and most convincing case histories of the P_1, P_2, P_3... sequence is the detailed description by Giedion of the series of designs by Linus Yale Jr between 1861 and 1865 which led to the lock which bears his name. His work continued some of the inventions of his father, who was also a locksmith. The most radical innovation probably arose from the use of a principle which was in evidence on the wooden locks of Pennsylvania Dutch barns, in turn derived from ancient locks which were known in many parts of the world.

What is true for the invention of complex machines holds equally true for the earlier development of tools. Most of the manual tools which have been in everyday use for long periods are in large measure modelled on some bodily action. Hammers, pliers, tweezers all perform more effectively and more powerfully the actions of our hands; the saw with its 'teeth' imitates the kind of ripping action we can

206 Mechanical Reaper
British Patent, 1811

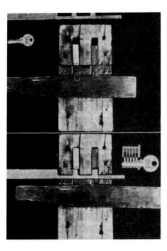

207 Pennsylvania Dutch Wooden Lock
top: locked, bottom: unlocked.
Yale key shown as comparison

achieve by moving an object between our teeth, and the vice clamps in the way we can grip with our teeth. The history of tools is surely a demonstration of one of the earliest uses of models and of the most readily available, namely the familiar actions of the designer.

In the case of radical mechanical inventions we see the result of a model shift. Instead of developing the scythe by improving the cutting blade (as indeed happened after 1811) or handle or altering the materials, there is a switch to two other models: propelling by means of horsepower and cutting by means of a rotating blade. It is the combination of these established methods in a new way which is of significance. A century and a half later there was a return to the idea of a rotating cutter. In the intervening period the technology of the two-stroke engine and of small electric motors had advanced to such an extent that the horizontally rotating blade became applicable to cutting grass: an innovatory lawnmower was produced. Such inventions are arguably very close to the kind of radical model shift which shows new insights in the solution of architectural problems, as discussed earlier, and which frequently initiates a stylistic change.

When a new machine is invented or goes through a major stage of development only a very few components may be new; the engine, the wheels and the handle of the lawnmower are all well established. What is new is the combination of the parts in order to achieve a small rotary cutter which will trim grass. A new building, however innovatory, equally does not depend on every one of its components being redesigned; as a rule we accept reinforced concrete or roofing tiles or ironmongery and simply set about composing a novel assembly of these elements. Quite apart from the problem of time which would be involved in designing every component of a building from scratch, and the likely cost and difficulties of having these manufactured, we would probably also lose the benefits of error elimination which have accumulated over the years. Radical design in the past has not depended on total novelty.

The process of architectural design as described by the sequence $P_1 \rightarrow TS \rightarrow EE \rightarrow P_2$ borrowed from Karl Popper's writings on science cannot claim to be unique to architecture. It seems safe to assume that the sequence holds good in many other fields of design, and that moreover the sequence with its underlying need for some historical models is a reasonable description of the design process, whether this results in work of acclaimed originality or more modest solutions. What is relevant is that this process has been used in architecture for centuries. It has therefore been applied to issues of considerable complexity which have had to consider interwoven questions of space usage, visual appearance, meaning, moral values, technology, human comfort, economy and an array of problems, some of which are always present while others vary from time to time. The buildings which have resulted from this process represent large parts of whole cultures and are the most visible evidence by which we relate to periods of history. Architecture not only provides one of the most basic needs, that for shelter, but is also the most tangible proof of the past; of the present as part of a continuity. At its best it is also a pointer to the future; it can, by a powerful celebration of the present, give us cause for optimism.

If the power and application of electronic technology increases in the future – as seems desirable and inevitable – and if one of the serious applications of that technology is to simulate the design process in its most general and widest sense, as has been suggested, it may be worth remembering that that process has been commonplace in architecture at a high level for at least four and a half thousand years. There is thus surely a new relevance to architecture and a new vital reason why we should understand its processes.

Notes

p. 1, line 5	Mills (1959)	p. 39, line 44	Echenique (1972)
p. 9, line 13	McCoy (1975)	p. 40, line 8	Echenique *et al.* (1971)
	Cardwell (1977)	p. 40, line 15	Martin & March (1972)
p. 11, line 38	Pevsner (1972)	p. 41, line 8	Pevsner (1976)
p. 12, line 2	Semper (1989)	p. 43, line 47	Pearsall & Salter (1973)
p. 12, line 28	Semper (1860/63)	p. 45, line 4	Münz & Künstler (1966)
p. 13, line 15	Lyons (1970)	p. 45, line 9	Le Corbusier (1923)
p. 13, line 33	Leach (1976)	p. 45, line 17	Wright (1958)
p. 14, line 8	Leach (1976)	p. 46, line 18	Banham (1962)
p. 14, line 18	Grabar (1973)	p. 46, line 32	Le Corbusier (1923)
p. 15, line 35	Vitruvius (1960)	p. 47, line 4	Wagner (1979)
p. 15, line 42	Alberti (1986)	p. 47, line 9	*The Shakers* (1974)
p. 16, line 5	Wittkower (1973)	p. 48, line 3	Wrede (1980)
p. 16, line 28	Palladio (1965)	p. 48, line 4	Caldenby & Hultin (1985)
p. 17, line 31	Rykwert (1972)	p. 48, line 5	Wilson (1988)
p. 19, line 16	Monod (1972)		Cruickshank (1988)
p. 22, line 9	Janik & Toulmin (1973)	p. 50, line 26	Norberg-Schultz (1963)
p. 22, line 19	Semper (1852)	p. 51, line 21	Alexander (1966)
p. 23, line 23	Schorske (1961)	p. 52, line 7	Summerson (1957)
p. 24, line 15	Münz & Künstler (1966)	p. 52, line 31	Banham (1960)
p. 26, line 15	Leitner (1973)	p. 53, line 25	Langer (1957)
p. 26, line 31	Schilpp (1974)	p. 54, line 4	Weeks (1963–64)
p. 26, line 47	Kraft (1974)	p. 54, line 20	Brawne (1970)
p. 27, line 17	Popper (1944/66)	p. 58, line 41	Pevsner (1948)
p. 27, line 20	Popper (1972/74)	p. 59, line 7	Popper (1972/74)
p. 28, line 25	Burnham (1941)	p. 60, line 5	Popper (1972/74)
p. 29, line 24	Magee (1973)	p. 60, line 36	Popper (1972/74)
p. 30, line 24	Popper (1944/66)	p. 60, line 46	Popper (1972/74)
p. 33, line 1	Kaufmann (1962)	p. 62, line 4	Popper (1972/74)
p. 34, line 47	Festinger *et al.* (1950)	p. 62, line 47	Feyerabend (1958)
p. 35, line 3	Newman (1972)	p. 63, line 20	Lakatos & Musgrave (1970)
p. 35, line 18	Rivlin *et al.* (1969/70)		
p. 36, line 47	Alexander *et al.* (1968)	p. 63, line 25	Kuhn (1962/70)

p. 63, line 35	Habermas (1972)	p. 118, line 30	Welsh (1971)
p. 64, line 21	Feyerabend (1970)	p. 119, line 35	White & White (1964)
p. 67, line 9	Schilpp (1974)	p. 121, line 28	Purdom (1949)
p. 67, line 25	Gombrich (1960/70)	p. 122, line 6	Fein (1972)
p. 69, line 32	Semper (1884)	p. 123, line 7	Bellamy (1888/1942)
p. 71, line 28	Reiner (1963)	p. 124, line 14	Gans (1967)
p. 72, line 20	Collins (1965)	p. 124, line 31	March (1967)
p. 75, line 5	Johnson (1947)	p. 132, line 33	Lip (1979)
p. 76, line 42	Greenberg (1975)	p. 132, line 44	Popper (1957/74)
p. 77, line 7	Wölfflin (1922/32)	p. 134, line 30	Tyng (1984)
p. 77, line 23	Gombrich (1960/77)	p. 135, line 9	Brawne (1963) & (1970)
p. 81, line 6	Henze (1963/66)	p. 135, line 42	Linstead *et al.* (1961)
p. 81, line 46	Kopp (1970)	p. 136, line 30	Mumford (1956)
p. 84, line 15	Vogt-Goknil (1966)	p. 137, line 10	Smithson (1972)
p. 85, line 11	Sylvester (1975)	p. 141, line 20	Hall (1969)
p. 86, line 13	Akhmatova (1975)	p. 149, line 11	Popper (1972/74)
p. 86, line 35	Willett (1971)	p. 152, line 16	Barthes (1964)
p. 90, line 4	Ruskin (1851–53)	p. 153, line 2	Bird (1976)
p. 91, line 14	Wittkower (1973)	p. 153, line 26	Hogben (1971)
p. 91, line 22	Snodin (1991)	p. 155, line 18	Colquhoun (1981)
p. 95, line 46	Rowe & Koetter (1975)	p. 158, line 14	Prown (1977)
p. 97, line 37	Jencks & Silver (1972)	p. 172, line 12	Johnson (1979)
p. 99, line 12	Brawne (1973)	p. 174, line 24	Brawne (1977)
p. 101, line 10	Venturi (1966)	p. 184, line 43	Brawne (1965)
p. 103, line 5	Popper (1972/74)	p. 187, line 26	Brawne (1973)
p. 103, line 39	Eisenmann (1972/75)	p. 202, line 8	Dal Co & Mazzariol (1986)
p. 105, line 5	Lasdun (1984)	p. 204, line 8	Lotz (1977)
p. 105, line 14	Laudan (1981)	p. 217, line 16	Giedion (1948/69)
p. 109, line 1	Kirsch (1990)		

Illustration credits

Every effort has been made to trace owners of copyright material but the author would be glad to hear from any copyright owners of material produced in this book whose copyright has unwittingly been infringed.

17 Leitner, B., *The Architecture of Ludwig Wittgenstein*, Studio International Publications; *18, 38* Reprinted with the permission of Macmillan Publishing Company from *Meaning in Western Architecture* and *Existence, Space and Architecture* by C. Norberg-Schultz, originally published by Studio Vista/Cassell & Company Ltd. © 1975; *19* Avery Library, Columbia University; *21–23* Prof. Christopher Alexander; *25* Benevolo, L., *A History of the City*, Scolar Press; *27* By permission of the British Library; *28, 57* Le Corbusier, *Towards a New Architecture*, Architectural Press; *31* Asplund, G., *The Dilemma of Classicism*, The Architectural Association; *36* Gombrich, E. H., *Art and Illusion*, Phaidon Press; *37, 50, 52, 108* © DACS 1992; *39, 40* Hederer, O., *Leo von Klenze*, Callwey Verlag; *41* Reprinted by permission of the publishers from *Space, Time and Architecture* by S. Giedion, Cambridge, Mass: Harvard University Press, © 1941, 1949, 1954, 1962, 1967 by the President and Fellows of Harvard College; *42* Courtesy of the Museum of Modern Art, New York; *43* © ADAGP, Paris/DACS, London, 1992; *45, 92–105 Wasmuths Monatshefte für Baukunst Vol. 1927*, Ernst Wasmuth AG; *46* © The Hedrich-Blessing Collection at the Chicago Historical Society; *47* Rudofsky, B., *The Prodigious Builders*, Secker and Warburg; *49* Prof. Hermann Lebherz; *51* Sherrard, P., *Athos, the Holy Mountain*, Sidgwick & Jackson; *59, 78* MacDonald, W., *Early Christian & Byzantine Architecture*, reprinted by permission of George Brazilier, Inc. © 1962; *66* © Staatliche Museen Preussicher Kulturbesitz, Kunstbibliothek, Berlin; *67, 72, 73, 79, 136 Architectural Review*; *70* Burkhardt, J., *The Architecture of the Italian Renaissance*, Penguin Books; *71* Courtesy of Electa, Milan; *74, 84* © Martin Charles; *75* Alvar Aalto, *Interior & Exterior Windows*, Alec Tiranti/Editions Girsberger; *80* Blaser, W., *Richard Meier: Building for Art*, Birkhäuser Verlag; *81* © Norman McGrath; *83* © Julie Phipps; *86, 150, 161* © Verlag Gerd Hatje; *87, 88* Le Corbusier, *Oeuvre Complete 1910–29*, Erlenbach; *113* Courtesy of the Ulster Museum; *114* Ardalan, N. and Bakhtiar, L., *The Sense of Unity*, University of Chicago Press; *115* Van Zanten, D., *Designing Paris*, MIT Press; *122* Le Corbusier,

References

Alberti, L. B., *The Ten Books of Architecture*, The 1755 Leoni Edition, Dover Publications, New York, 1986

Alberti, L. B., *On the Art of Building in Ten Books*, (translated by Joseph Rykwert, Neil Leach and Robert Tavernor), MIT Press, Cambridge, Mass., 1988

Alexander, C., *The City as a Mechanism for Sustaining Human Contact*, Center for Planning and Development Research, University of California, Berkeley, California, 1966

Alexander, C., 'From a set of forces to a form', in *The Man-made Object*, Gyorgy Kepes (ed.), Studio Vista, London, 1966

Alexander, C., Ishikawa, S. and Silverstein, M., *A Pattern Language which Generates Multi-Service Centers*, Center for Environmental Structure, Berkeley, California, 1968

Alexander, C., Silverstein, M., Angel, S., Ishikawa, S. and Abrams, P., *The Oregon Experiment*, Oxford University Press, New York, 1975

Alexander, C., Ishikawa, S., Silverstein, M., *A Pattern Language: Towns, Buildings, Construction*, Oxford University Press, New York, 1977

Alexander, C., *The Timeless Way of Building*, Oxford University Press, New York, 1979

Alexander, C., *The Linz Cafe*, Oxford University Press, New York, 1981

Alexander, C., *The Production of Houses*, Oxford University Press, New York, 1985

Alexander, C., Neis, H., Anninou, A. and King, I., *A New Theory of Urban Design*, Oxford University Press, New York, 1987

Akhmatova, A., 'Amadeo Modigliani', in *The New York Review of Books*, 17 July 1975

Banham, R., 'Vitruvius, go home' (vote of thanks by Sir John Summerson), *Architectural Association Journal*, London, March 1960

Banham, R., *Theory and Design in the First Machine Age*, Architectural Press, 1962

Barthes, R. and Martin, A. (photographer), *La Tour Eiffel*, La Génie du lieu No. 4, Paris, 1964

Bellamy, E., *Looking Backward, 2000–1887*, Random House, New York, 1888/1942

Bird, A., *Paxton's Palace*, Cassell, London, 1976

Brawne, M., 'Approaches to residential planning', *Architectural Review*, London, October 1963

Brawne, M., *The New Museum*, Architectural Press, London, 1965

Brawne, M. (ed.) 'The new universities', *Architectural Review*, London, April 1970

Brawne, M., 'Aalto at Aalborg', *Architectural Review*, London, March 1973

Brawne, M., 'What is wrong with eclecticism', in *Gottfried Semper und die Mitte des 19 Jahrhunderts*, Birkhauser-Verlag, Basel, 1976

Brawne, M., 'Art gallery extensions', *Architects' Journal*, London, 30 November 1977

Brawne, M., 'Geoffrey Bawa', *Architectural Review*, London, April 1978

Brawne, M., *The Museum Interior*, Thames and Hudson, London, 1982

Burnham, J., *The Managerial Revolution*, Penguin Books, Harmondsworth, 1941/1945

Caldenby, C. and Hultin, O., *Asplund*, Arkitektur Verlag, Stockholm, 1985

Cardwell, K. H., *Bernard Maybeck: Artisan, architect, artist*, Peregrine Smith, Santa Barbara and Salt Lake City, 1977

Collins, P., *Changing Ideals in Modern Architecture*, Faber and Faber, London, 1965

Colquhoun, A., *Essays in Architectural Criticism: Modern architecture and historical change*, MIT Press, London, 1981

Cruickshank, D. (ed.), 'Erik Gunnar Asplund', *Architects' Journal*, London, 1988

Dal Co, F. and Mazzariol, G., *Carlo Scarpa: the Complete Works* (translated by R. Sadleir), Architectural Press, London, 1986

Echenique, M., Anthony, J., Baxter, R., Crowther, W., Lindsay, W. and Perraton, J., *Urban Systems Study: Report 1967–70*, Land Uses and Building Form Studies Report No. 2, Cambridge, 1971

Echenique, M., 'Models: a discussion', in *Urban Space and Structures*, L. Martin and L. March (eds), Cambridge University Press, Cambridge, 1972

Eisenmann, P., *Five Architects: Eisenmann, Graves, Gwathmey, Hejduk, Meier*, Oxford University Press, New York, 1972/1975

Fein, A., *Frederick Law Olmsted and the American Environmental Tradition*, George Braziller, New York, 1972

Festinger, L., Schachter, S. and Bach, K., *Social Pressures in Informal Groups*, Harper and Brothers, New York, 1950

Feyerabend, P. K., 'An attempt at a realistic interpretation of experiences', *Proceedings of the Artistotelian Society*, London, Vol. 58 (1957–8), 1958

Feyerabend, P. K., 'Consolations for the Specialist', in *Criticism and the Growth of Knowledge*, I. Lakatos and A. Musgrove (eds), Cambridge University Press, London, 1970

Gans, H., *The Levittowners: Ways of life and politics in a new suburban community*, Allen Lane, London, 1967

Giedion, S., *Mechanization Takes Command*, W. W. Norton, New York, 1948/1969

Gombrich, E. H., *Art and Illusion*, Phaidon Press, Oxford, 1960/1977

Grabar, O., *The Formation of Islamic Art*, Yale University Press, New Haven, Conn., 1973

Greenberg, C., 'Seminar Five', *Studio International*, London, May/June 1975

Habermas, J., *Knowledge and Human Interests* (translated by J. J. Shapiro), Heinemann, London, 1972

Hall, E. T., *The Hidden Dimension: man's use of space in public and private*, Bodley Head, London, 1969

Henze, A., *La Tourette*, Lund Humphries, London, 1963/1966

Hesse, M., *The Structure of Scientific Inference*, Macmillan, London, 1974

Hogben, C., *Art-deco: French decorative arts in the twenties*, Victoria and Albert Museum, London, 1971

Howard, E., *Garden Cities of Tomorrow*, Swan Sonnenschein, London, 1902

Janik, A. and Toulmin, S., *Wittgenstein's Vienna*, Simon and Schuster, New York, 1973

Jencks, C. and Silver, N., *Adhocism: The case for improvisation*, Secker and Warburg, London, 1972

Johnson, P. C., *Mies van der Rohe*, Museum of Modern Art/Simon and Schuster, New York, 1947

Johnson, P. C., *Writings*, Oxford University Press, New York, 1979

Kaufmann, E. Jr., 'Frank Lloyd Wright's Fallingwater 25 years after', *L'architettura*, Milan, August 1962

Kaufmann, E. Jr, *Fallingwater: Frank Lloyd Wright Country House*, Architectural Press, London, 1986

Kirsch, K., *The Weissenhofsiedlung: Experimental housing built for the Deutscher Werkbund, Stuttgart, 1927*, Rizzoli International Publications, New York, 1990

Kopp, A., *Town and Revolution: Soviet architecture and city planning 1917–1935* (translated by T. E. Burton), Thames and Hudson, London, 1970

Kraft, V., 'Popper and the Vienna Circle', in *The Philosophy of Karl Popper*, P. A. Schilp (ed.), Part 2, Open Court, La Salle, Illinois, 1974

Kuhn, T. S., *The Structure of Scientific Revolutions*, Chicago University Press, Chicago, 1962/1970

Kuhn, T. S., 'Logic of discovery or psychology of research?', in *Criticism and the Growth of Knowledge*, I. Lakatos and A. Musgrave (eds), Cambridge University Press, London, 1970

Lakatos, I. and Musgrave, A. (eds), *Criticism and the Growth of Knowledge*, Cambridge University, Press, London, 1970

Langer, S. K., *Problems of Art*, Routledge and Kegan Paul, London, 1957

Lasdun, D. (ed.) *Architecture in an Age of Scepticism*, Heinemann, London, 1984

Laudan, L., 'A problem-solving approach to scientific progress', in *Scientific Revolutions*, I. Hacking (ed.), Oxford University Press, Oxford, 1981

Leach, E., *Culture and Communication*, Cambridge University Press, Cambridge, 1976

Le Corbusier, *Towards a New Architecture* (*Vers une architecture*, 1923, translated by F. Etchells), Architectural Press, London, 1946/1971

Le Corbusier, *Journey to the East* (edited and translated by I. Zaknic), MIT Press, Cambridge, Mass., 1966/1989

Leitner, Bernhard *The Architecture of Ludwig Wittgenstein*, Studio International Publications, London, 1973

Linstead, P., Barnard, G. A. and McCreath, M., '1,800 students of science and technology: a survey of the Imperial College', *Universities Quarterly*, London, December 1961

Lip, E., *Chinese Geomancy*, Times Books International, Singapore, 1979

Loos, A., *Spoken into the Void: Collected essays 1897–1900*, (translated by J. O. Newman and J. H. Smith), MIT Press, Cambridge, Mass., 1982

Lotz, W., *Studies in Italian Renaissance Architecture*, MIT Press, Cambridge, Mass., 1977

Lyons, J., *Chomsky*, Fontana, London, 1970

Magee, B., *Popper*, Fontana/Collins, Glasgow, 1973/1979

MacDougall, E. and Ettinghausen, R. (eds) *The Islamic Garden*, Dumbarton Oaks, Washington, 1976

March, L., 'Homes beyond the fringe', *RIBA Journal*, London, August 1967

Marino, de S. and Wall, A., *Cities of Childhood: Italian Colonie of the 1930s*, Architectural Association, London, 1988

Martin, L. and March, L. (eds) *Urban Space and Structure*, Cambridge University Press, London, 1972

McCoy, E., *Five California Architects*, Praeger Publishers, New York, 1975

Mills, C. W., *The Sociological Imagination*, Oxford University Press, New York, 1959

Monk, R., *Ludwig Wittgenstein: The duty of genius*, Jonathan Cape, London, 1990

Monod, J., *Chance and Necessity* (translated by Austryn Wainhouse), Collins, London, 1972

Mumford, L., *The Human Prospect*, H. T. Moore and K. W. Deutsch (eds), Secker and Warburg, London, 1956

Murphy, R., *Carlo Scarpa and the Castelvecchio*, Butterworth Architecture, London, 1990

Münz, L. and Künstler, G., *Adolf Loos: Pioneer of modern architecture*, Thames and Hudson, London, 1966

Newman, O., *Defensible Space: People and design in the violent city*, Architectural Press, London, 1972

Norberg-Schultz, C., *Intentions in Architecture*, Universitetsforlaget/Allen and Unwin, 1963

Palladio, A., *The Four Books of Architecture*, Dover Publications, New York, 1965

Pawley, M., *Theory and Design in the Second Machine Age*, Blackwell, Oxford, 1990

Pearsall, D. and Salter, E., *Landscapes and Seasons of the Medieval World*, Paul Elek, London, 1973

Pevsner, N., *An Outline of European Architecture*, John Murray, London, 1948

Pevsner, N., *Some Architectural Writers of the Nineteenth Century*, Clarendon Press, Oxford, 1972

Pevsner, N., *A History of Building Types*, Thames and Hudson, 1976

Popper, K. R., *The Open Society and its Enemies*, Vols 1 and 2, Routledge and Kegan Paul, London, 1944/1966

Popper, K. R., *The Poverty of Historicism*, Routledge and Kegan Paul, London, 1957/1974

Popper, K. R., *The Logic of Scientific Discovery*, Hutchinson, London, 1959/1975

Popper, K. R., *Conjectures and Refutations*, Routledge and Kegan Paul, London, 1963

Popper, K. R., *Objective Knowledge*, Oxford University Press, London, 1972/1974

Prown, J. D., *The Architecture of the Yale Center for British Art*, Yale University Press, New Haven, Conn., 1977

Purdom, C. D., *The Building of Satellite Towns*, Dent, London, 1949

Putnam, H., 'The corroboration of theories' in *Scientific Revolutions*, I. Hacking (ed.), Oxford University Press, Oxford, 1981

Reiner, T. A., *The Place of the Ideal Community in Urban Planning*, University of Pennsylvania Press, Philadelphia, 1963

Rivlin, L. G., Proshansky, H. M. and Ittelson, W. H., 'Changes in psychiatric ward design and patient behavior', *Transactions of the Bartlett Society*, Vol. 8, 1969–70 School of Environmental Studies, University College, London

Rowe, C. and Koetter, F., 'Collage City', *Architectural Review*, London, August 1975

Ruskin, J., *The Stones of Venice*, Smith and Elder, London, 1851–53

Rykwert, J., *On Adam's House in Paradise*, The Museum of Modern Art, New York, 1972

Schilpp, P. A. (ed.), *The Philosophy of Karl Popper*, Parts 1 and 2, The Open Court, La Salle, Illinois, 1974

Schorske, C., *Fin-de-Siècle Vienna: Politics and culture*, Cambridge University Press, Cambridge, 1961/85

Semper, G., *Der Stil in den technischen und tektonischen Künsten oder praktische Ästhetik*, Vols 1 and 2, first edition 1860/63, second edition 1878/79, Friedrich Bruckmann's Verlag, Munich

Semper, G., *Kleine Schriften von Gottfried Semper*, M. and H. Semper (eds), Berlin & Stuttgart, 1884

Semper, G., *Wissenschaft, Industrie und Kunst*, 1852; reprinted, H. M. Wingler (ed.), Neue Bauhausbücher, Mainz, 1966

Semper, G., *The Four Elements of Architecture and other Writings* (translated by H. F. Mallgrave and W. Herrmann), Cambridge University Press, Cambridge, 1989

The Shakers: Life and production of a community in the pioneering days of America, catalogue of travelling exhibition, Neue Sammlung, Munich, 1974

Smithson, A. and P., 'Robin Hood Gardens', *Architectural Design*, London, September 1972

Snodin, M. (ed.), *Karl Friedrich Schinkel, a universal man*, Yale University Press, New Haven, Conn., 1991

Summerson, J., 'The case for a theory of modern architecture', *RIBA Journal*, London, June 1957

Sylvester, D., *Interviews with Francis Bacon*, Thames and Hudson, London, 1975

Taylor, B. B., *Geoffrey Bawa*, Mimar/Concept Media, Singapore, 1986

Tyng, A., *Beginnings: Louis I. Kahn's philosophy of architecture*, John Wiley and Sons, New York, 1984

Unwin, R., *Nothing Gained by Overcrowding!*, Garden Cities and Town-Planning Association, London, 1912

Venturi, R., *Complexity and Contradiction in Architecture*, The Museum of Modern Art/Doubleday, New York, 1966

Vitruvius, *The Ten Books of Architecture* (translated by M. H. Morgan), Dover Publications, New York, 1960

Vogt-Goknil, U., *Living Architecture: Ottoman*, Oldbourne, London, 1966

Wagner, O., *Die Baukunst unserer Zeit*, 1914; quoted in Geretsegger, H. and Peintner, M., *Otto Wagner 1841–1918*, Academy Editions, London, 1979

Wasmuth Monatshefte für Baukunst, XI Jahrgang, Verlag Ernst Wasmuth, Berlin, 1927

Weeks, J., 'Indeterminate architecture', *Transactions of the*

Bartlett Society, Vol. 2 1963–64 University College, London

Welsh, A., *The City of Dickens*, Clarendon Press, Oxford, 1971

White, M. G. and White, L., *The Intellectual versus the City: from Thomas Jefferson to Frank Lloyd Wright*, New American Library, New York, 1964

Willett, F., *African Art*, Thames and Hudson, London, 1971

Wilson, C. St J., *Gunnar Asplund 1885–1945: The dilemma of classicism*, Architectural Association, London, 1988

Wittkower, R., *Architectural Principles in the Age of Humanism*, Academy Editions, London, 1973 (first published 1949)

Wölfflin, H., *Principles of Art History* (translated by M. D. Hottinger), Dover Publications, New York, 1922/32

Wrede, S., *The Architecture of Erik Gunnar Asplund*, MIT Press, Cambridge, Mass., 1980

Wright, F. L., *The Living City*, Horizon Press, New York, 1958

Index